To Migs and John
with authors
Compliments

John O' Callaghan

A Bit Of The Blarney

5/15/01

Jokes And Anecdotes
Guaranteed To Make You Smile

By
John J.O'Callaghan
Ireland's International Comedian

GW00721836

Published by

Post Offi... ...c. East Plaza,
S... ...78

John & Jeanette O'Callaghan
8332 Barton's Farm Blvd.
Sarasota, FL 34240

Published by
Hot To Trot, Inc.
Post Office Box 14081, North East Plaza,
Sarasota, Florida 34278

**Library of Congress Catalog Card Number:
92-97028**

ISBN 1-882255-00-3

Need Extra Copies For Your Friends?
Call Toll-Free Anytime And Use Your Credit

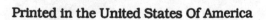

Printed in the United States Of America

A Bit Of The Blarney

Sheila

Eugene Ramsbottom, an Irishman who owns a sheep farm in Waga-Waga, in the Australian outback claims to have invented the first ever perfume specially formulated for Aussie bush women. He's named it "Sheila," sells it in bulk, and claims it's a great bargain at only $10.00 a half gallon. Not only does it help to make the women sexually irresistible, he says, but when diluted, it makes a great sheep dip and also kills flies.

Unfaithful Twice

When I returned home after a long overseas visit I asked my wife if she had ever been unfaithful during my absence. She said, "I was unfaithful twice. Once with the crew of the Q.E.2., and once with the members of the local golf club."

The Pet Pig

I once stayed in a bed and breakfast place in Mullingar, Ireland. When I went down to breakfast, the landlady told me that there was a pan of breakfast porridge on the stove and that I was to help myself. So I picked up this blue and white enamel bowl off the table and helped myself. As I was eating my breakfast her pet pig came up to where I was sitting at the table and went "Oink! Oink!" as if it was begging for some of my porridge. I said politely, "That's a very friendly little pig you've got there Missus."

"I'm not so sure about that, sir," the landlady said, "I think he's just a wee bit jealous 'cause you're eating your porridge out of his little blue bowl."

Her Third Husband

I went into a Dublin pub for a Happy Hour drink, and sat next to a very attractive young woman. I asked if I could buy her a drink and after three gin and tonics she became very friendly, moved her stool closer to mine and said,

"You know, you look very much like my third husband."

So I said, "How many husbands have you actually had?"

"Two," she said giving me a broad come-on smile.

Supporting A Family

I asked my girl friend's father if I could marry his daughter, and he said,

"Are you able to support a family?"

"Yes sir," I said,"I have a very good job with prospects."

"Think carefully now," he said, "there's three of us?"

Mrs. O'Houligan's Ass

Legend has it that if you sit long enough in the fashionable Horse Shoe Bar in Dublin's Shelbourne Hotel in St. Stephen's Green, you'll meet everyone you ever knew. And it was there that I bumped into Mike Murphy. We were enjoying a noggin and a natter and when Murphy took off his cap, I could see he had a lump on the top of his head as big as a ducks egg. He saw me looking at the lump and said,

"Hardman O'Houligan did it."

"Good God," I said, "he must have been holding a brick in his hands to have caused a lump as big as that?"

"He was holding a golf club," Murphy said,

"And what were you holding in your hands at the time?" says I. "Mrs. O'Houligan's ass," Murphy said.

> *"The trouble with this singles bar is that men come in looking for a one-night stand, and the women come in looking for a commitment."*

The Compatibility Test

Shortly after I joined Noah's Ark Mating and Dating Agency I was introduced to a very attractive divorcee. On the first date she told me she liked romantic things like classical music and intimate candlelight dinners for two. I told her I did too.

"I also like foreign travel. I like walking on the beach. I like good books. I like bridge. I like old time dancing," she said,

"So do I," I replied.

"How about sex?" she enquired.

"Infrequently," I said.

"Is that one word or two?" she cheekily asked.

That's Italian

I was trying to impress my new girl friend so I took her to Luigi's Italian restaurant. I looking at the menu, made my selection and said to the waiter in my best Italian accent, "Bonus Noches Camarero. A glass of Chianti Classico Dolce por favor, the Caesar salad, and for the entree I'll have the Spondilini Pescadora, with some extra Parmesan and lots of garlic."

"Excuseh Senor," the waiter said, "but isa no a Spanish restaurante, and Spondilini Pescadora isa da name offa da chef."

Jehovahs Witness

A door-to-door missionary called on my mother and asked if she'd like to be a Jehovahs Witness.

"Don't know him," she said, "and I never even saw the accident."

The Sex Quiz

I have a friend who is a professor at University College, Dublin. He was on a TV game show where if you answered a question correctly, you won a lot of money. It was his third week and he had already answered questions on quantum physics and genetic engineering. You only got 24 hours notice of the question, but you could, if you wished, confer with an expert of your own choosing. To win $100,000.00 my friend had to answer three questions on sex. And so he decided to have me with him on the show as back-up.

"Imagine," the quiz-master said when we were on stage,"that you have to turn a woman on. For $100,000.00, in what three places would you kiss her?"

"On the lips," the professor said.

"Correct," said the quiz-master.

"On the neck, just below her right ear," the professor said.

"Correct," said the quiz-master "and the third place?"

My friend turned to me and raised his eyebrow questioningly. "Don't look at me," I said, "I've been wrong twice so far."

The Fighting Irish

I remember being shaved by a Dublin barber with a very shaky hand. After losing nearly half a cup of blood I stood up and asked if I could borrow a straight razor.

"Are you going to try and shave yourself sir?" he enquired. "No," I said, "but I'd like to be able to defend myself."

The Psychology Of Stress

I was staying at the Midland Hotel, New Street, Birmingham, England, on business. Before dinner, I went into the cocktail bar for a happy hour drink. I immediately spotted a gorgeous green-eyed blonde with a model face and an hourglass figure. She was sitting on a bar stool provocatively swinging her lovely long legs and looking as if she was bored. So I sat on the stool next to her and politely asked if I could buy her a drink. She slowly looked me up and down and then shouted,

"NO. I WILL NOT SLEEP WITH YOU." Everybody was staring at us so I lowered my voice to a whisper, and said,

"I was just trying to be friendly and sociable."

"YOU WANT TO DO WHAT?" she screamed at the top of her voice. By this time I was so confused and embarrassed that I didn't know quite what to say. So I hurriedly backed away as fast as I could, and went into the restaurant to have dinner. The restaurant was very crowded but they found me a table, and just as I was about to order, I looked up and saw her talking to the head waiter and pointing at me. I tried to hide behind the menu, but she came over, stood by my table and said,

"Sir, I feel I owe you an apology. I'm a psychology student and I am doing a field test on how different people react under stress." And in a very loud voice I said, "TWO HUNDRED DOLLARS?"

> "Call her an opera singer? That old bag couldn't even play the part of the caterpillar in Madame Butterfly."

Priest Wanted Urgently

I was on this train travelling to Limerick when a guy from the next carriage stuck his head in the doorway of ours and said,

"For God's sake, is there a Catholic priest in here?" There wasn't, and he went away. But a few minutes later he was back, and he said,

"Is there a Protestant minister in here?" There wasn't, but this little guy stood up and said,

"Can I be of assistance? I am a Baptist minister."

"No," the man replied. "I only want to borrow a corkscrew."

> *"It took her ages to persuade him to buy her a new mink coat, and when she finally got it, she was too big to wear it."*

A Very Close Shave

There was a very pretty manicurist at the barber's so I decided to have my nails manicured in the hope of chatting her up.

"I think you're simply gorgeous," I said, "and I was wondering if you'd care to have dinner with me this evening and maybe we could see a show or go dancing afterwards?"

"You'll have to get my husband's permission first," she said, "and you can ask him now, because he's the one who's shaving you."

Bob Peters

I went to a new barber and a Jewish guy came in and said,

"Bob Peters here?"

"No," the barber said, "we are only licensed to cut men's hair."

Aer Lingus

I once worked as a pilot for Aer Lingus. On my first Dublin-New York flight I was over Kennedy Airport when I was asked to state my height and position. "I'm five foot twelve inches," I said, "and I'm sitting in the front seat."

The Brothel

In Limerick where I grew up, I used to play in a street where one of the houses was used as a brothel. At that time I thought a brothel was some kind of restaurant that only served soup. However I noticed that all the customers were men and that when they went in they looked hungry and unhappy, and when they came out, they were always smiling. There was no printed menu outside so I and one of my school playmates decided to question one of the customers as he was coming out.

"Hey mister," I said, "What do they give you to eat in there and how much does it cost?"

"It costs me $50.00 each time, son, but I can tell you that you wouldn't like it. It's for grown-ups only."

"How much spending money have you got?" I asked my friend. "I have got two quarters," he said.

"And I've got two quarters," I said. So together we climbed up the steps to the brothel, rang the bell and were greeted by a big busty woman with red hair. She was wearing an off-the shoulder blouse, a short tight-fitting black leather skirt and white knee-high boots.

"What do you kids want?" she said.

"Please missus," I said, "we'd like to know what can we get for a dollar?" The madam never said a word but she suddenly grabbed both of us and banged our heads together. Then she kicked our asses down the steps, went inside and slammed the front door shut. After we picked ourselves up off the sidewalk and dusted ourselves down, I turned to my friend and said,

"We are lucky we only had a dollar, 'cause I think if we had $50.00, she'd have murdered the pair of us."

The Gospel Of Getting On

When I was first left my home in Ireland, to look for work in England, my father gave me this advice:

"Son, beware of anyone who tries to tell you something is free, because nothing ever is. And when you do get a job, remember these three things:

#1. Wear a bright red shirt.
#2. Do more than you are paid to do.
#3. Save ten percent of everything you earn.

The bright red shirt will help to get you noticed. Giving good value and service is the best way to win friends and influence people, so try to always leave the other fellow in your debt.

Save ten percent of everything you earn. Loan the money to the bank, and when you re-invest the interest, you'll get a higher return due to the magic of compound interest.

Money in the bank gives you leverage. With a good credit rating you can borrow money at favourable terms. When you use this borrowed money as a deposit on land and houses, you will be acquiring assets that are likely to appreciate in time. Whereas the purchasing power of money is likely to depreciate, because of inflation.

When you're rich and a man of property, everyone will want to know you and call you friend. But when you're poor and only have a couple of pennies left, the hustlers of this world will even try to wheedle those out of you.

Determine to be your own boss as soon as you can and put your money out to work for you, instead of you having to go out to work for it. As a businessman, you'll have to learn how to take the calculated risk. Be cautious. The trick is to only bet on situations where you personally are in a position to effect the outcome. But be aware that it is quite possible to lose more than you actually wager; and that the unfortunate man who loses his shirt, soon finds he loses most of his friends as well.

🍀

You can be anything you want to be, provided your goal is realistic, and in keeping with your talents. You must believe in yourself, son. As soon as you know exactly what you want, go for it; confidently expecting to succeed more than you expect to fail. Determine to succeed, and persist until you do. Begin to think and act now, as if you already are, the successful person you know you will be. If you can visualise it, you can realise it. If you can believe it, you can achieve it. For, more often than not, the man who succeed in life, is the man who believes he can."

> *"Tall, dark and handsome?" she said. "Huh! The only way you'd look tall is if you stood on a chair. And the only way you might be mistaken for handsome is in the dark."*

Linda Lovelacy

"What's new?" Casey said to Murphy when they met in the pub.

"I'm getting married next week," Murphy said.

"What's she like?" his friend asked.

"She's a right little cracker. And I can't believe my luck. She's got red hair, lovely skin, a big bust, nice ass and great legs."

"What's her name?"

"Lovelacy."

"Surely it isn't Lovely Linda Lovelacy who used to live in Ballyfriggin?"

"The very same," Murphy replied, "Have you heard of her then?"

"Not only have I heard of her," Casey said, "She's the proverbial good time that was had by all the lads in the village. In fact we used to refer to her as the village bike."

Murphy thought about that for a moment and said,

"Well, sure Ballyfriggin's not that big a place."

Blaming The Dog

When Murphy got engaged, Linda, his fiancee invited him home to dinner for the first time. Brussels sprouts and onions were served with the meal and this gave Murphy a lot of wind in his stomach. After dinner he was sitting by the fire and the family dog lay curled up at his feet. Murphy thought that if he broke wind quietly the dog would get the blame. Shortly after he had done so, his mother-in-law-to-be, scowled at the dog and shouted,

"Get up Rover." But the dog ignored her. Feeling rather pleased with himself, Murphy again broke wind and again she shouted, "Get up Rover." The dog never moved. When Murphy broke wind for the third time, she became very agitated, stood up, kicked Rover and shouted,

"Get up-get up, before he shits all over you."

"You will be careful, darling, won't you?"

Murphy's Pet Parrot

When Murphy announced he was getting married his pet parrot threw a fit and insisted on going on honeymoon with them.

"OK," Murphy said to the parrot, "You can come, but I don't want you looking. Promise you'll look the other way when we're making love, and if you break your promise, you'll get no food." The parrot readily agreed and kept his face turned toward the wall all night as the happy couple made love. In the morning as he was packing their suitcase, Murphy said to his new wife,

"I can't get it all in, Linda. You'll have to sit on it. No, that's no good either," he said, "I'll get on top and press down. No," he said, "I still can't do it that way, but I have an idea. Why don't we both get on top?" And the parrot said, "Food or no food, this I gotta see."

The Shortest Day

Mrs. Murphy woke at 7 a.m., got out of bed, put on her bra, her panties and her dressing gown, took the cover off the parrot cage, opened the window drapes, went down to the kitchen, made some coffee, and the phone rang. It was her husband Mike who said,

"Linda, darling, I've just got off the plane. Keep the bed warm and I'll be there in about an hour."

So Mrs. Murphy went back upstairs, took off her dressing gown, took off her bra and panties, closed the drapes, covered up the parrot, and got back in bed. And the parrot said, "Jay-sus. That was a short day."

A Change In Attitude

When Casey first got married, he weighed three hundred and fifty pounds, and his wife only weighed one hundred and twenty five. On the wedding night, he took off his pants, threw them at his new wife and in a commanding voice said,

"Put them on, wench."

Thinking it was some kind of game, she climbed into the pants and said,

"I can't possibly wear these, Pat?"

"Quite so," he said, "and let that be a lesson to you, I wear the pants in this house." A little while later, she took off her flimsy panties, threw them to him and said,

"Put them on."

"I can't possibly get into these, honey," he said. And she said, "No, and you won't, until you change your attitude."

Finnigan's Cafe

A couple of Brits were on vacation in Ireland and staying in the attractive town of Dun Laoghaire, County Dublin. They were in a cafe having an argument over the name of the town.

"It's pronounced Done Lock Aire," he said,

"No. It's Dune Leery," she said,

Finally the husband called the waitress over, and said,

"Help us settle an argument, Miss, tell us, how do you pronounce the name of this place?" And the waitress said,

"F-I-N-N-I-G-A-N-S C-A-F-E."

Big Willie

Big Willie won first prize in a waiters competition at the Blue Nose Nudist Club in Skerries, County Dublin. He was the only one able to carry two cups of coffee and eight doughnuts at the same time.

A Ghost Story

Murphy was coming home late after a night out with the boys. It was midnight and he decided to take a short cut through the cemetery. He heard an owl hoot and the screeching of bats as they swooped on an unlucky nocturnal field mouse and ate it. There was a full moon and he could clearly read the names of the dead carved on their marble tombstones. Suddenly he heard an errie "Clink-Clink" like steel on stone. It made his skin creep and the hair on the back of his neck stand up on end. "Clink-Clink" it went again. The sound appeared to be coming from the front of a large white marble tombstone.

---- 🍀 ----

Murphy approached the tombstone very, very slowly. Eventually he plucked up enough courage to peep around the the stone - and was astonished to see a man kneeling on the grave with a hammer and a chisel in his hands.

"Oh my God," exclaimed Murphy, "you nearly frightened the life outa me. But why are you working here at twelve o'clock at night?" And the man said,

"The stupid stone mason spelled my name wrong."

The Partners Confessions

Marvin Goldburger and Louie Stephanski had been partners in a rag trade business for years and as Stephanski lay on his death bed, he sent for his partner.

"You remember that time the IRS audited your personal accounts? Well it was me who fingered you."

"I know Louie," Goldburger said quietly.

"And do you remember that time you were on the road for six months and when you came back your wife was four months pregnant, and she wouldn't tell you who the father was? Well it was me who made her pregnant."

"I know, I know," Goldburger said, and his voice was filled with emotion and there were tears running down his cheeks.

"And do you remember that time someone bought your mortgage and then foreclosed on you? Well it was me."

"I know," Goldburger said, and his voice was just a whisper.

"I know how you hate dirty tricks," Stephanski said, "but we were partners for a very long time. Can you ever forgive me?"

"Yes," said Goldburger, "I forgive you, but I too have to ask your forgiveness, Louie. You see it was me who poisoned you."

The Wrong Name

Casey telephoned his friend Murphy and said,

"Do you remember when you went on that deep sea fishing holiday last year, Mike, and you stayed with that widow who kept a bed and breakfast place at Salthill in Galway Bay?"

"Yes," said Murphy.

"Did you sleep with her?"

"I did," said Murphy.

"And did you by any chance give her my name?

"I did," said Murphy laughing, "and I gave her your address as well. It struck me as very funny at the time, but how did you find out?" And Casey said, "Because she's just died and left me the bed and breakfast place."

"His blind wife's now left him. The mean
bastard flattened the Braille in her book."

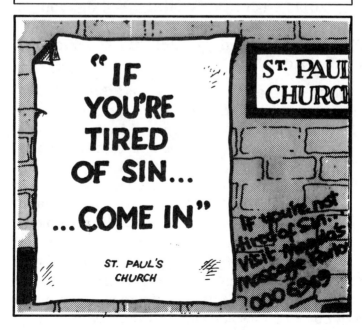

The Mail Order Bride

Hardman O'Houligan met his first wife through an ad in the Saturday Rendezvous singles column of the London Times. The courtship was entirely by correspondence and he agreed to marry her sight unseen. He paid her fare over to Ireland and when she got off the bus at Ballyfriggin, he was to say the least, a bit disappointed. He loaded her and her luggage onto his donkey and cart and as they set off on the journey to his farmhouse, the donkey stumbled. O'Houligan got very annoyed and said,

"That's one."

They went about a mile and the donkey stumbled again. "That's two," he said.

They went another mile and again the donkey stumbled. "That's three," O'Houligan said, pulled out his gun and shot the donkey dead. His English bride-to-be was so shocked she screamed at O'Houligan.

"You stupid Irish twit. What the hell did you do that for?"

O'Houligan scowled, pointed his finger at her and said, "That's one."

> "She had seven husbands, and three of them were her own. She always said she doesn't mind her men loving her and leaving her, so long as they leave her enough. She says she's only 39, but her twin sister is 49. The secret of her success with men can be summed up in just one word. "Yes." She even said to my own brother, "Don't get married. Take it from me."

Second-Hand Tombstone Bargain

Ad in the Personal column of a Dublin newspaper:
"Green Connemara Marble Tombstone. Used once only. Great bargain for someone named O'Toole."

The Aphrodisiacs That Worked

Mrs. Goldburger went to Dr. O'Flannel, told him her husband Marvin seemed to have lost interest in sex and asked for a prescription that might work.

"I've just about tried everything," she said, "I've fed him on chicken soup and matzo balls, oysters and ginseng, garlic and vitamin E capsules. I've even given him snake soup laced with yeast that a Chinese friend recommended. I've even massaged his private parts with olive oil, red pepper and Aloe Vera, but the only rise I ever get out of him is when he gets up out of bed to go for a pee."

"I've got samples of a new pill that's just come out," the doctor said, "the manufacturer's rep swears by them. Try popping one of these in his Ovaltine just before he goes to bed. The effect is supposed to be immediate. Come back and tell me what happened next week." The following week Mrs. Goldburger saw the doctor again and said,

"There's good news and bad news, doctor. I was so desperate I dropped three pills into his after dinner cup of coffee when he wasn't looking. The effect was immediate. He leaned across the table right there and then and said,

'Beccy, something is rising up and I have this uncontrollable urge to have sex with you right this very minute.'' Then he pulled me down on the floor, jumped on top of me and screwed me right there under the table. It lasted for two whole minutes and it was the best sex I've had in years. And it would have lasted longer, if the owners of the restaurant hadn't thrown the pair of us out."

> "You might think four feet six inches is not very tall, but when my Sean is standing on his wallet, he looks six foot six to me."

Our Son The Doctor

Mrs. Stephanski died, went to heaven and had a great time talking to Moses and all of the other great Old Testament prophets. Eventually she got to meet with St. Joseph and The Blessed Virgin Mary.

"Speaking as a mother myself," Mrs. Stephanski said, "I know how proud you must be of your wonderful son, but tell me, weren't you just a little bit disappointed when he didn't go into the family business as a carpenter?"

"What happened was God's own will," the Blessed Virgin Mary said, "but I have to admit that for a while we were hoping he might become a doctor."

At The Dentist

Miss Apprehension went to the dentist and as he was bending over her to give her an injection he suddenly exclaimed in horror,

"Miss Apprehension," he said, "I know you're nervous but are you aware you are holding me by the testicles?"

"I know Doctor," she said, "and we're not going to hurt each other, are we?"

The Dog Who Played Bridge

Three cats needed a fourth for a game of bridge so they asked the next door neighbour's dog if he would join them.

"I didn't know your neighbour's dog was a good bridge player?" one cat whispered to the other.

"He's not," the cat said, "Every time he gets a good hand he wags his tail."

> *"They called him 'Jack The Pint Killer,' but just before he died, he went delirious. He kept asking for water."*

Poison Mushrooms

Hardman O'Houligan and a friend were talking over a few jars of ale and O'Houligan mentioned that both of his wives were dead.

"How did your first wife die?" The friend enquired. And O'Houligan replied,

"She ate poison mushrooms."

"And how did your second wife die?" the friend asked.

"A crack in her skull," O'Houligan said.

"Wow!" exclaimed the friend, "how did that happen?"

"She wouldn't eat the mushrooms."

Mass For A Dead Dog

Pat Casey's dog died and he went to see Father O'Flynn, and asked if the priest would say mass for his beloved dead dog.

"Sorry, I only say masses for people," Father O'Flynn said. "But there's a New Age church just opened down the road and they may be able to provide some kind of a prayer service."

"Thanks Father," said Pat, "but do you think $200.00 will be too small an offering to give them?" And Father O'Flynn said,

"Now why didn't you tell me right away that your dog was Catholic?"

Whores And Boxers

"There are only two kinds of Irish that come over here from Ireland, and that's whores and boxers," the drunk at the bar in the English pub proclaimed to his drinking companion His drinking companion said,

"Steady on old man, I find that remark highly offensive. My wife happens to be Irish." Sobering up very quickly the drunk said, "And what weight does she fight at?"

Losing His Sex Drive

Mike and Linda Murphy hadn't been married long when Linda went to see Dr.O'Flannel and complained that her husband Mike was seemingly losing his sex drive.

"And when did you first notice this Mrs. Murphy," the doctor enquired. And she said, "Late last night doctor, and again first thing this morning."

Rule Britannia

An Englishman died and went to heaven and St.Peter said, "What were you doing just before you died?"

And the man said, "I had a few drinks but I clearly remember walking down O'Connell Street in Dublin singing Rule Britannia at the top of my voice."

"And when was that?"

"Within the last sixty seconds," the man said.

Casey's Complaint

Casey went into a pharmacy in the next village and said to the lady behind the counter,

"It's a bit embarrassing, but what can you give me for a permanent erection?"

"Just a moment sir," she said, "I'll have to go in the back and ask my sister." When she came out she said,

"I've spoken to my sister and she says I am to offer you full board and lodging and $200.00 a week."

The Loud Mouth Butcher

Mrs. Murphy and Mrs. Casey were chatting and Mrs. Murphy said, "The new butcher has an extremely loud voice."

"What did you say?" replied Mrs. Casey, adjusting her hearing aid.

"I said the new butcher shouts and bawls like a bull."

And Mrs. Casey said, "Has he?"

How To Save A Quarter Million

The smart new sales assistant said to his boss, "Do you want to save a cool quarter of a million dollars, sir?"

"How?"

"Is it true that when your only daughter marries, you'll give her a dowry of half a million dollars?"

"Yes."

"Well, I'd be willing to marry her for half that amount."

> "I went to the Church Singles dance and the only man I fancied there was the priest."

Saving His Ass

Casey couldn't find any odd jobs to do in Ireland so he took his beloved donkey over to England and they went from door to door looking for work. Jobs were scarce and the only offer of employment he got was from the vicar of a Protestant church, who said he could clean the church every day. Casey asked the vicar if he would allow his donkey to eat grass in the parish field adjacent to the church, and the minister readily agreed. Pat was happy in his work and regularly went to mass at the Catholic church across the road. The vicar's wife noticed this and complained to Pat about his apparent lack of loyalty. Pat said,

"The reason I go to the Catholic church is to save my soul, and the reason I go to your church is to save my ass."

To Hiss In Their Pit

The baby snake came in crying and said to the mammy snake,

"The snakes next door won't let me hiss in their pit".

And the mammy snake said,

"I knew them when they didn't have a pit to hiss in. You go over there when it's dark and you can hiss all over their pit."

A Love Bite

"I don't like the new governess," young Liam Lynch said to his mother, "and the next time she's nasty to me, I'm going to pinch her on the ass, and bite her on her chest, like daddy does."

Sean O'Shian's Wake

Sean O'Shian died. The wake was held in the house and the neighbors for miles around came to pay their respects. After the mourners had spoken to his mother, the eldest son noticed they seemed shocked at whatever his mother said, so he decided to listen in to the next conversation.

"Och I'm so sorry for your trouble. He was a fine man," he heard a neighbor say to his mother, " And what did he die of?"

"He died of the gonorrhea," she said.

The eldest son hurriedly approached his mother and said,

"Mother! Me da didn't die of the gonorrhea like you are saying. He died of the diarrhoea - a different thing altogether."

"Sure I know the difference son," she said, "but I'd rather your da was remembered as a bit of a sporting gentleman, instead of the auld shit he really was."

Not Catholic
Goldburger was knocked down by a bicycle and as he got up, a Catholic acquaintance who was passing by, saw him bless himself with the sign of the cross.

"Since when did you become a Catholic, Marvin?"

And Goldburger replied,

"You know I'm not Catholic. I was just checking my spectacles my testicles, my wallet and my pen."

Three Chairs
At Sean O'Shian's Wake, the lads had placed his coffin on top of an antique dining table sitting in the front parlour. Suddenly there was a terrible creaking sound and one of the table legs gave way and the coffin crashed to the floor and poor auld Sean fell out. Three of the lads lifted him back in again and one said,

"Wouldn't it be safer if we got three chairs and put the coffin up on that?" His friends thought it a good idea and so he turned around and as everyone was sitting down, he said,

"Could we please have three chairs for poor auld Sean?"

And all the mourners stood up and chanted, "Hip. Hip. Hooray."

Her Little Schnauzer
Mrs. Murphy's dog had too much hair in its ear so she asked the new pharmacist for some hair remover.

"What's it for?" he asked.

"It's for my little schnauzer," she said.

"Apply it very carefully three times a day," he told her, "It might irritate your skin, so better not ride your bike for a week."

☘ Casey's Ass

Casey came home drunk one night. All the lights were out and his wife was in bed asleep. He took off his shoes and quietly went up stairs. Half-way up he tripped and fell, and broke the half bottle of whiskey he had in his trousers back pocket. He went to the bathroom, dropped his pants, looked at his backside in the mirror and saw that it was cut and bleeding in several places. He opened the first aid box, and looking in the mirror, he carefully stuck Band-Aids over the cuts on his ass. He then sneaked into bed without waking his wife. Next morning Mrs. Casey woke her husband and said,

"You came in drunk last night, fell and cut your ass."

"How did you know?" he said in amazement.

And she said, "I heard you fall down the stairs, and this morning went I looked in the bathroom mirror, there were Band-Aids stuck all over the mirror."

The Coffee House Sugar Tongs

A little old unmarried lady complained to the manager of a Dublin City centre coffee house frequented by young business executives, that she had observed the men run in, run to the bathroom, run out, get in line, pick up a coffee and using their fingers, then pick up one or two lumps of sugar out of the bowl on the counter. So she complained to the manager.

"It's unhygienic," she said. "Obviously these young men are in too much of a hurry to even wash their hands. They rush straight out and then they handle the sugar lumps we all have to use. You ought to provide a pair of tongs." The manager said he would see to it. But after a week there was still no sugar tongs to be seen. She protested again and the manager took her into the gentlemen's bathroom and proudly showed her a set of tongs attached to a chain alongside each urinal.

The Second Coming

When the Irish Prime Minister was voted into office for the third time, a compositer at a Dublin newspaper set the headline 'CHARLIE'S BACK' in letters three inches tall. On seeing this the editor frowned and said,

"I was saving that big type for the second coming of Christ."

Herpes

This lady died and when she got to heaven St Peter said, "What was the cause of death?" And she replied, "Herpes." And St. Peter said,

"You don't die of herpes." And she said,

"You do if you give it to Hardman O'Houligan."

Lot's Wife

Father O'Flynn was teaching Bible class, and said, "And God told Lot to take his wife and flee from the city and not look back. And Lot's wife looked back and was turned into a pillar of salt." And one little boy said,

"Please Father, and what happened to the flea?"

A Bit On The Side

A big guy used to stick his head in the doorway of a barber's shop and say,

"Are there many ahead of me?" And the barber would say, "There's 4 or maybe 5. But I can take you in about 2 hours?" The fellow always said, "I'll come back later," but never did. After about 6 months of this the barber got very curious and said to his young assistant,

"Next time that queer fella comes in, follow him and tell me where he goes to get his hair cut." So the young assistant followed him and when he returned said,

"He goes to your house."

The Tortoise And The Snail

A snail was raped by a tortoise. The snail pressed charges and her attorney said,

"In your own words, please describe the incident to the court."

"It's hard to describe," the snail said, "it all happened so fast."

> *"He was wearing a kilt and when I asked him what was under it, he said, 'I'm a man of few words, dearie, gimme your hand.'"*

The Golfer's Psalm

He maketh my ball to lie in the green pastures of the fairway. He leadeth it around the still water hazards. Yea, though I walk through the rough, I will fear no bogey, for He hath prepareth the green before me, and marked the presence of sand traps. Truly my putt runneth over to the cup, and dwells within, and my name shall be engraved on the championship cup for ever.

The Elephant And The Monkey

After the final holocaust the only living creatures were a female elephant and a male monkey.

"If we don't procreate," the monkey said to the elephant, "the world will end with us two."

"But how would we get together?" the elephant asked. And the monkey said,

"I'll climb up his coconut tree, swing from the branches, and you back into me". The elephant agreed, but backed in too far, hit the tree and knocked a coconut off, which fell on her head.

"Ouch," the elephant said. And the monkey said,

"Sorry darling."

A Jewish Housewife's Dilemma

Sign in a butchers shop window:

"Pork chops 50% off. Buy One - Get One Free."

Motivational Murphy

Murphy got a job as a copywriter for the Dublin advertising agency, Flim, Flam, Adcon, Hustle and Bamboozle. Shortly afterwards he met his old friend Casey who had fallen on hard times and was reduced to begging for handouts on O'Connell Bridge, Dublin.

"How ya doin' Pat?" Murphy asked.

"Terrible," Casey said. "I've been holding this big sign up in front of me all day that says 'Laid-off at 50. Wife and seven hungry children and a sick donkey to support. Please give generously.' And all I can say about generosity in Dublin is that it's conspicuous by its absence."

"It's the wrong message," Murphy said. "When you want a Dubliner to open his or her wallet or purse, you have to appeal to their heart, not to their head. Let me rewrite the message for you." And he did and Casey was delighted with the public's response to his appeal. The message Murphy had written simply said,

"SPRING IS COMING....

BUT I SHAN'T SEE IT."

A Mink Coat From Harrod's

Marvin Goldburger was on safari in Borneo, where he was captured by a tribe of head hunters. They were about to cut off his head and cook him, when the chief said,

"Since you are obviously a sporting gentleman, I'll give you two choices. It's the pot, or you marry my oldest daughter." Goldburger looked at her and saw she was grossly overweight, was tattooed from head to foot, had an ivory bone going in one nostril and out the other, and her ear lobes had become elongated from wearing lumps of solid gold weighing about one pound each. He shook his head and politely said, "She's not quite my type."

"Pity about all that dowry going to waste," said the chief.

"Dowry," said Goldburger, "you never mentioned the dowry before. What is it?"

"Five thousand acres of rain forest, a gold mine and an opal mine."

"Oy, gevalt!" Goldburger said, "When's the wedding?" He took her on an around-the-world trip for their honeymoon. They were in Knightsbridge, London and passing Harrod's store when Goldburger said,

"I'd like to see you in a mink coat," and in they went. She tried on hundreds of coats, and eventually found one big enough to fit her. As she was looking at herself in the mirror, wearing the mink coat, the bone through her nose

and the huge chunks of gold hanging from her ears, Goldburger could see that she didn't like the coat.

"You don't like?" he said shaking his head.

"No, Marvin," she said, "I think mink makes me look far too Jewish."

> *"He picked up so much wet change from bar counters, he got rheumatism in his fingers."*

The Lost Weekend

Murphy did so well at the advertising agency where he worked that he won an all-expenses paid weekend in New York. He toured all the Irish pubs, got drunk and woke up in a hotel bed lying between two women, both of whom were still asleep and snoring. The one on his left was middle-aged, quite ugly and grossly overweight, and the one on his right was about eighteen, very slim and very beautiful. He had no idea who they were, nor how he got there. All he wanted to do was escape without waking them so he decided he would climb over the young one. He threw his leg over and as he was looking down on her, she immediately opened her eyes, looked up at him and exclaimed, "No! No! I'm the bridesmaid."

Green School Kids

A guy from Belfast, Northern Ireland, moved to America and got a job driving a school bus. About half the kids on the bus were white and the other half were black. Fighting broke out on the bus everyday and all hell was let loose. He put up with the fighting for 3 days and on the fourth day he stopped the bus and ordered everybody out. He lined them all up, told them he was from Northern Ireland

and that the main reason he came to America was to get away from people who were unable to settle their differences without fighting.

He then walked down the line and said to the first kid who happened to be black "You're not black. You're green."

The next kid happened to be white and so he said to him, "You're not white. You're green too."

He did that all the way down the line and told every kid that they were neither black nor white but green. Finally he said,

"OK. Now that's settled, I want everyone back on the bus in an orderly way. Pale green to the front. Dark green to the rear."

The New Company Logo

Three large Irish insurance companies were having talks about a possible amalgamation. Anticipating that the merger would go through, Mr. Flim of Flim, Flam Adcon and Bamboozle Advertising Agency decided to make a pitch for the account. He asked Murphy to dream up a new logo. He was perplexed when he saw the illustration. It showed a circle divided into three sections. Inside each section was a drawing of a man and woman coupled together in bed. He asked Murphy for an explanation, and Murphy said,

"The first section shows a man in bed with a hooker. That's COMMERCIAL UNION. The second shows a man in bed with his secretary. That's EMPLOYERS LIABILITY. The third is a young man in bed with his girl friend. And that represents MUTUAL TRUST."

A Gay Dwarf Irishman

There's a hotel in London's West End that's known for catering to the whims of some of the world's richest and most eccentric clients. After checking in this guy phoned room service, gave his room number and said,

"Send me up 2 high class hookers - a blonde and a redhead, a bottle of cold-pressed extra virgin Italian olive oil, 8 pieces of rope 3' long, a saddle and a whip, a number 3 golf club and a gay dwarf Irishman." Two hours later the clerk phoned and said,

"Sorry about the delay, sir, but I have now assembled in the lobby, the 2 high class hookers - a blonde and a redhead, the bottle of cold-pressed extra virgin Italian olive oil, the 8 pieces of 3' long rope, the saddle and the whip, and of course the number 3 golf club. But I am very sorry to tell you that we couldn't find a gay dwarf Irishman. However, we did manage to locate a gay dwarf Englishman. Will he be satisfactory sir?" And the guy said, "No. He won't do at all. Cancel the whole thing. I'll have a dry martini instead."

A Kiss From Murphy

Murphy's advertising agency boss sent him to see an important client in the little town of Ballyfriggin. He was obliged to stay overnight. The only hotel, The Ballyfriggin Arms Hotel was completely full.

"I have one spare bed in a double room," the landlord said "but there's a man in the other bed and I'm afraid he snores like a pig all night long. I'm afraid you wouldn't get much sleep."

"I'll take the bed," Murphy said. Next morning the landlord asked Murphy how he had slept.

"Like a log," Murphy.

"And didn't the other fella snoring bother you?"

"He didn't snore at all," said Murphy, "although right enough he was snoring when I first went in, but after I woke him with a big kiss, he stayed awake all night watching me."

The Masked Fancy Dress Ball

Lord Goolie and his wife were invited to a masked fancy dress ball at a friend's manor house on New Years Eve. They had decided to wear Batman and Batwoman costumes, but Lord Goolie had to go alone, as at the last minute Lady Goolie was confined to her room with another one of her migraine attacks. Shortly after he had gone she began to feel better and decided to attend the party after all, dressed not as Batwoman, but as The Fairy Queen. When she got to the party, she saw her handsome husband in his Batman outfit, surrounded by a bunch of lovely ladies. She joined the throng. and although Lord Goolie didn't recognize her, he flirted outrageously with her. She wondered just how far he would go, and without saying a single word, she wickedly enticed him upstairs and into one of the guest bedrooms. He didn't say a word either and immediately after they had sex, she left the ball, went home, got into bed and waited for her husband.

"Did you have a nice time darling?" she sweetly enquired.

"No, my dear," he said, "I had a most dreadfully boring evening." And she said "Really?"

"I left the ball almost immediately" he said, "and went to the club and played bridge with three of the other bored husbands. I lent my costume to Carruthers and apparently he had a great time. He said he screwed some old bag dressed like a Fairy Queen."

♣

The Prostitution Business

Rosie and Roxanne, two street walkers and old friends from way back, but who hadn't seen each other for many years, met on a street in Dublin's red light district.

"How's business then?" enquired Rosie.

"I am kept very busy," replied Roxanne, "In fact there's so much business about, if I had another pair of legs, I'd open up in Belfast."

Mrs. Casey's Sore Thighs

Mrs. Casey wasn't very tall and she was also seriously overweight. She went to the doctor and told him that the tops of her fat thighs become very chafed and sore, especially when she went upstairs. The doctor listened sympathetically and gave her a prescription for 3 things. A bottle of aspirin, a jar of Vaseline and a can of talcum powder. Just as she was leaving he shouted after her.

"Oh by the way Mrs. Casey, I nearly forgot but there's one more thing. When you get home I would strongly advise you to cut at least six inches off the tops of your Wellington boots."

The Yellow Rolls Royce

A guy bought the latest top-of-the line Rolls Royce and as he was driving it home from the showroom, he stopped at a traffic light. As he was waiting for the lights to change, a guy in a very old yellow Rolls Royce drew alongside and indicated he wanted to speak to the guy in the new Rolls.

"New car eh?" he said. "How do you like the quadrophonic sound?" The guy in the new Rolls said he didn't have quadrophonic sound, and went back to the dealer and said,

"Look here, I've just paid all this money and a guy in an old Roller made me feel embarrassed because he has quadrophonic sound and I don't. I want you to install quadrophonic sound immediately." A few days later he again met the guy in the yellow Rolls who shouted to him,

"How do you like watching CNN and HBO on your TV?" He was forced to admit he didn't have TV fitted, so he went straight back to the dealer and said,

"I can't be shown up like this. I want you to fit every conceivable extra regardless of price." A few days later the guy in the new Rolls happened to see the yellow Rolls parked at a rest area, with the windows all steamed up. So he stopped his car, got out, went up to the yellow Rolls, and tapped on the glass window. The guy inside wound the window down one inch and said, "What is it?" The other guy said,

"I have just phoned my bankers in Geneva on my car phone and reception was as clear as a bell." And the guy in the yellow Rolls said angrily,

"Do you mean to say you got me out of my sauna just to tell me that?"

The Skiing Champion

After winning the Swiss cross-country skiing championship in Geneva, Murphy was being interviewed live by the Radio Telefis Eireann outside broadcast team.

"Tell the people back home Mr.Murphy," the interviewer said, "what was the first thing you did when you met your wife Linda back in your Swiss hotel after winning the championship?" And Murphy said, "I'd rather you asked me the second thing."

"OK. What was the second thing?" And Murphy said, "I took off my skies."

The Birds and The Bees

Casey called his teenage son in from the backyard where he was playing baseball with his younger brother and said,

"Your mother said now that you are thirteen it's time I told you all about the facts of life." So in an embarrassed roundabout way, Casey told his son about the mating habits of the birds and bees.

"Now you go and tell your younger brother what you've learned," he said. When the eldest son got outside he said to his young brother,

"You know what you and me was doin' with the twins 'round the back of the bicycle shed last week? Well dad told me to tell you that the birds and bees do the same thing."

The Mailman's Last Day

It was the mailman's last day before retiring and he called on Mrs. Shananegin to deliver a registered packet.

"I know this is your last day," she said, "Come on in. Follow me. I've got a lovely surprise for you." So she led him into the kitchen, sat him down at the table and served him with the best breakfast he had ever had. Then she took his hand and without saying a word, led him upstairs and into the master bedroom. She threw herself on the bed, and pulled him down on top of her. After they had sex she leaned across to where her purse was on the bedside table, opened it, took out two dollars and pushed it into the astonished mailman's hand.

"Oh, no," he said, "you've been too generous already. I can't take money as well."

"Ah but you must," she insisted, adding, "it's my husband's idea."

"Yes," she said. "Last night when we were talking after dinner I told him it was your last day and I said, 'What do you think I ought to give him', and Seamus said, 'Oh screw him. Give him a couple of dollars.' But I want you to know the breakfast was entirely my idea."

Not A Member Of The Club

Casey was playing a round of golf with a friend who was learning to play. As they were about to tee off, the friend said,

"I've got to pee. I can't wait. Is it ok if I pee on the grass?" And Casey said,

"No. No. You'll ruin the green. Go over there and pee through the bushes." Just then there were three ladies walking up the driveway to the Golf Club when they saw this thing sticking through the bushes.

"Tut-tut-tut," one said, "I think that's really disgusting."

"I'm glad it's not my husband," the second one said. And the third one said, "He's not even a member of the Club."

Murphy's Long Willie

Murphy went big game shooting in Africa and was attacked by a man-eating lion. He managed to fight off the lion but not before the lion had bitten off his left ear, a chunk out of his elbow and the end off his willie. The natives found him and took him to their village where the local witch doctor performed some emergency spare part surgery. He gave Murphy an antelope's ear. He patched up his elbow with some muscles from a gorilla's elbow, and then he stitched part of an elephant's trunk on to the end of Murphy's willie. Murphy recovered. Three years later he was even better than before and so he went back to Africa to thank the witch doctor for having saved his life.

"With my antelope's ear," he said "I can hear a feather fall. With my gorilla's elbow I've won the local tennis club championship three times, and with my extra long willie, I'm a big hit at cocktail parties - especially when they pass the peanuts."

Casey's Goose

Casey went to play Bingo and won a live goose. On his way home he was passing the cinema and noticed that there was a film on he had wanted to see. He decided to conceal the goose and tucked it down inside the front of his trousers. While he was engrossed with what was happening on the big screen, the goose stuck it's head out of his fly. A young lady sitting next to Casey saw the goose's head waving about, nudged her lady companion and said,

"Get a look at this". And her friend said,

"Naw. If you have seen one, you've seen 'em all". And her friend said, "Yes, but this one's eating my popcorn."

Undressing For The Doctor

Miss Fortune went to see Dr. O'Flannel and said she was embarrassed about the size of her big boobs and protuberant nipples. He told her to remove all her clothes as he was going to give her a full examination.

"I feel a bit embarrassed about taking off all my clothes in broad daylight," she said, "I wonder if you would mind switching off all the lights and closing the drapes?" He agreed and when she was ready she called out,

"I'm completely naked now Doctor. Where shall I put my clothes?" And he said, "You can throw them on the floor on top of mine."

It's A Small World

There were these two friends playing golf and their game was held up by two ladies at the hole ahead.

"I'll drive down in the cart," one said, "and see if I can hurry them along." But half-way down, he suddenly turned the cart around and came back.

"I just got a terrible shock," he said, "one of those ladies is my wife, and the other's my mistress."

"I'll go," his friend said, and half way down he turned back. "What a small world it is," he said.

The Leprechaun's Pussy Willows

The new golfer's ball went off the green and landed in a bunch of buttercups. He made several attempts to get the ball out but only succeeded in slicing the tops off the buttercups. Suddenly a little leprechaun jumped out and said,

"You have vandalised my lovely buttercups and my curse is that for a year you won't be able to enjoy eating butter." When he told his partner about the leprechaun's curse, his partner said,

"Margarine's not so bad. You're lucky you didn't slash his pussy willows."

Salmonella Poisoning

Mrs. Murphy decided to give a dinner party for her husband's posh advertising agency bosses and their wives, and had bought and cooked a whole salmon. A few minutes before the guests arrived she went in the kitchen and saw the cat was up on the table and had eaten a hunk out of the side of the salmon. She opened a tin of salmon, mixed it with mayonnaise and used it to plaster up the hole, which she then covered with slices of cucumber.

Everyone said the salmon was wonderful, but when she went in the kitchen to make the coffee, she found her cat lying dead by the back door. She called Mike in to the kitchen, showed him the dead cat and said, "It must be the salmon." When the unhappy couple confessed what had happened, the partners Flim, Flam, Adcon and Bamboozle nearly had a fit. One of them telephoned the paramedics and an ambulance came and took them all to hospital where they had to suffer the trauma and indignity of having their stomachs pumped out. But nobody died and next day a neighbor called on Mrs. Murphy and said, "Linda, I'm so sorry about your cat. I found it dead in the street. A car must have hit it, and not wanting to disturb your party, I put the dead cat inside your kitchen door."

The Antique Dealer's Cat

An English antique dealer was scouting around the junk and antique shops on Dublin's Quays in search of Georgian furniture. He spotted a kitten in the window of one shop drinking milk out of what he recognized as a Ming Dynasty porcelain bowl. He went in and pretended to examine a few pieces of furniture. As he was leaving the shop, he told the shop keeper there was nothing that took his fancy, but added that he'd like to buy the kitten as a gift for his young daughter.

The shop owner wanted $100.00 for the kitten and the English dealer readily agreed, and then slyly added,

"What about throwing in the kitten's old milk bowl as well?" And the antique dealer said,

"Ah no sir. That's my lucky bowl. It helps me sell all the kittens I can get my hands on."

The Optimistic Advertiser

"Healthy 55-year-old thirsty bachelor with corkscrew wishes to meet sex-starved deaf and dumb widow who owns a pub."

Murphy's Two Black Eyes

Murphy had two black eyes and when Casey asked how he got them he said,

"It's hard to believe, but I got them in church when I was at 11 o'clock mass last Sunday. There was a fat lady in front of me wearing a silk dress. When she stood up her dress got caught in the cheeks of her bottom. Being a gentleman, I reached over with my finger and thumb, and carefully pulled it out. She must have felt me doing it because she suddenly turned around and hit me in the eye."

"But you have two black eyes, Mike?"

"Hardman O'Houligan came in late and sat beside me. When we stood up to sing the hymn, her dress got caught again in the crease of her ass, and before I could stop him, O'Houligan leaned over and pulled her dress out. 'No, no,' I said, 'She likes it tucked in.' And so I tucked in it, and she turned around and hit me in the other eye."

The Widow's Mite

Father O'Flynn asked the new young curate what he intended to talk about in his Sunday sermon.

"The Widow's Mite," he replied. Father O'Flynn had a twinkle in his eye as he said,

"After hearing the widows of this parish confess their sins for the last 20 years, 1 can tell you they all do."

Saints And Sinners

Father Greene, the late parish priest of Ballyfriggin, died and went to heaven. St. Peter met him at the pearly gates and said,

"Just a moment, Father, while I look up your record in the Book of Life. Hmmn," he said, "I see you never committed a single sin, but not only that, from the time you made your first communion at age six, you've done one good deed after another for almost everybody you met. In fact you're a saint. But the bad news is that the saint's section is full. The only room left is in the sinner's section, and I can't put you in because of all those good deeds you've done. However, since your case is so special, I am going to delay your death and send you back down to Ballyfriggin, where you'll have 30 minutes to commit a sin, repent and be saved."

Suddenly Father Greene found himself back in Ballyfriggin and he began to think of what kind of sin he could commit. At first he thought of stealing but then he remembered how a certain spinster in the village, a Miss Take, had always had the hots for him, so he decided he would call on her.

"Hello, Father," she said, "What a lovely surprise. I had heard you weren't too well but you're looking great. Come on in." So in he went and to cut a long story short, he went to bed with Miss Take and really enjoyed, what was for both of them, a first time sexual experience. Father Greene delayed his departure until the 30 minutes were nearly up and then he said,

"Miss Take, I hope you'll forgive me? I feel I have taken advantage of my position and our friendship, and used your body for my own selfish needs. Can you ever forgive me?"

"Ah not at all Father," she said, "sure 'tis I who should be thanking you for the good deed you've done today."

The Manor House Fire

Lord Chumperly left his wife in charge of the estate and told her he was going to Borneo for six months to catch butterflies. He tried telephoning home on numerous occasions but always failed to get through. As a last resort he tried telephoning the resident head gardener Pat Casey, who lived in the gate lodge on the estate.

"There's bad new and there's good news, your Lordship. Which would you like first?"

"Give me the bad news first," Lord Chumperly said.

"Your wife's run off with the chauffeur, sir, and they have taken the Rolls with them."

"OH MY GOD," Lord Chumperly exclaimed.

"And your favorite hunter is dead, sir."

"How did the horse die?"

"I'm not quite sure," Pat said. "Maybe it was the smoke from the fire?"

"FIRE! What fire?"

"The fire in the Manor House, sir."

"GOOD GRIEF! How did the fire start?"

"It must have been the candles around the coffin, sir?"

"WHAT CANDLES? WHOSE COFFIN?"

"When your wife left you it was a great shock to your mother, sir, and she died of a heart attack. The wake was held in the great hall, sir, and there were a lot of candles around the coffin. The window was open and a wind must have blown the curtains toward the candles, and maybe that's how the fire started?"

"And what about all my antique furniture, my silver, my old master paintings, my priceless rugs and my Persian carpets?"

"All gone sir. It was an awful big blaze, sir."

"For God's sake, man, give me the GOOD news." And Pat said,

"The heat from the fire brought the daffodils out early."

The Weakling Son

Big John had seven sons, six of whom were over six feet tall and very strong with blue eyes and jet black wavy hair, whereas the seventh was rather a wimpy weakling with brown eyes, blonde hair and only 5' tall. As John lay on his death bed he called his wife and said,

"Molly. I want you to tell me something. Even though I love all my sons dearly, I've always been a wee bit suspicious about that youngest one. Before I die, I want you to put my mind at rest. Tell me honestly now, am I really that fella's father?" Molly took his hand and said,

"Yes darlin'. He's yours alright. It's the others who aren't."

> *"I haven't had sex for six months, three weeks and two hours - and I hardly ever think about it."*

Lady Chumperly's Game Keeper

Shortly after her husband left on his extended trip to Borneo, and before she ran off with the chauffeur, the oversexed Lady Chumperly called the head game keeper to her study and said,

"Tarquin, please take off my shoes and my silk stockings." Feeling very embarrassed, Tarquin sheepishly said,

"Yes m'lady."

"Now take off my dress." Tarquin slowly peeled off her dress.

"Now take off my bra and my panties." Very slowly, Tarquin unhooked her bra and pulled her panties down.

"Now Tarquin," Lady Chumperly said, waving her finger at him, "Don't let me ever catch you wearing any of my clothes again."

Murphy's Dilemma

Murphy had two telephone calls. One from his wife who said she was feeling very romantic and would he hurry home. The other from one of his advertising agency colleagues inviting him over to share a couple of dozen bottles of Guinness.

A Cure For Constipation

Lord Chumperly didn't last long after the big fire and his wife running off with the chauffeur. A week before he died, he went salmon fishing and stayed at a small and very exclusive gourmet hotel in a rather isolated spot on the west coast of Ireland. He drank and ate overmuch, became constipated and quite ill. He never liked doctors so he asked the owner of the hotel if she could recommend anything. She referred him to the local vet and he told Lord Chumperly he always recommended castor oil for constipated calves, and said it worked very well for them. A week later the vet met the hotel owner and asked her if Lord Chumperly had been able to go to the bathroom. "Oh, yes," she said, "He went twice before he died, and three times afterwards."

Only 3 Days To Live

Mulligan came back from a visit to the Doctor looking very worried.

"I've got angina," he told his wife, "The doctor gave me these little pills and said I would have to take one every day for the rest of my life."

"That's no big deal," his wife said, "Angina won't kill you, so what are you looking so worried about?" And Mulligan said, "He only gave me 3 pills."

Mother's Milk

Casey went to see Dr. O'Flannel complaining about his stomach. Tests showed that Casey had developed an ulcer. Dr. O'Flannel proscribed a bland diet, but after three months Casey was still complaining about his stomach pains.

"A mother's milk might do the trick," Dr. O'Flannel said, and told Casey he would ask one of his patients, Mrs O'Toole, whose baby was unable to drink her milk, whether she might be able to help.

"I'll tell her it's a matter of life or death," he said. Mrs. O'Toole agreed and as Casey lay in her arms suckling her breast, she began to enjoy the sensation and said,

"Isn't there anything else you'd like Pat? Anything at all? My husband's at work and won't be home until after six." And Pat said, "Could I have a couple of crackers?"

No Sex

Mulligan had another heart attack and his doctor advised him that he had better totally abstain from ever having sex again as the excitement would probably kill him. The doctor put him on medication, recommended a low-calorie fat-free diet and told him he should try and walk for up to one hour each day. Mulligan did and after six months he felt like a new man. His doctor gave him a stress test and said he was amazed at his progress.

"It's amazing," he said, "you're in great shape. Your cholesterol is 150. Your blood pressure's 125 over 65 and the good news is that you can now go home and fulfil all Mrs. Mulligan's sexual desires and not be the least bit worried about your heart."

"Ah sure she'll never believe me," Mulligan said,

"I'll write you out a note that'll convince her," And he wrote:

Dear Mrs. Mulligan,
I have thoroughly examined Moriarty Mulligan, the bearer of this note, and I am pleased to confirm that he is in great physical shape and capable of having sex every day if need be.
Brian O'Flannel. MD.

Mulligan read the note but something was clearly bothering him.

"Is there a problem?" the doctor enquired.

"Yes," said Mulligan, "Would you ever mind crossing out 'Dear Mrs. Mulligan,' and instead put 'To Whom It May Concern.'

Great Expectations

Before he became parish priest in Ballyfriggin, Father O'Flynn taught at the local girls high school.

"Miss Cellany," he said to one young girl, "based on what we talked about yesterday, I want you to tell the class what part of a man's body is capable under certain conditions, of enlarging to ten times it's normal size, and describe those conditions?" Miss Cellany blushed bright red, and said,

"I'm too embarrassed to say, Father." Several young ladies in the class raised their hands, and turning to one he said,

"Yes, Miss Appropriate?"

"The pupil of a man's eye is capable of a ten times enlargement in the dim light," she said. Father O'Flynn turned back to Miss Cellany and said,

"I have three things to say to you Miss Cellany. #1. You weren't paying attention to yesterday's lesson. #2. You have a dirty mind. And #3, one of these days you are going to get married, go on honeymoon, and you are going to be very disappointed."

Singles Advertisement

"Bachelor with 3 roomed unfurnished apartment wishes to meet single lady with own furniture. Please send photograph of the furniture."

The Poor Collection

The priest was addressing the packed congregation from the pulpit at the eleven o'clock Mass one Sunday morning.

"As I announced earlier," he said, "the second collection at today's Mass was supposed to be for the poor of the parish, but after taking a quick look in the collection basket, I can see you are all here."

Four Children

Mrs. O'Toole said she never wanted any children but ended up having four. She called the first two Adolf and Rudolf, and the last two Get Off and Stay Off.

Three Tickets To Pittsburgh

A Catholic bishop, a monseigneur and a young priest arrived at the bus station intent on travelling to Pittsburgh.

"You buy the tickets father," the bishop said to the young priest, "and we'll keep a eye on the luggage." The ticket clerk was a very attractive buxom young woman. The first three buttons of her blouse were undone and a

substantial portion of her ample bosom was on display. The priest couldn't help but notice her charms. He began to feel a bit hot under the collar, and in his confusion blurted out, "Three pickets to Tittsburgh please." He immediately went red in the face and hurrying away. He explained the cause of his embarrassment to the bishop. The monseigneur said he would buy the tickets but when he got to the counter he too couldn't take his eyes off the buxom young lady. He became quite confused and couldn't even remember why he was at the counter. Putting his hands in his pockets, he found a dime, pulled it out, placed it on the counter and said,

"Can you give me two nipples for a dime please, miss?" Finally the bishop approached the counter, wagged an admonishing finger at the young woman and said,

"If you don't cover yourself up young lady, when you get to heaven, St. Finger will wag his Peter at you."

"Beccy, I said a 'Rich' Doctor!"

Painting The Porch

Casey was working as a painter and he called on a house in a posh suburb and asked the man if he had any painting jobs he'd like doing. The man gave Casey a gallon of paint and said,

"Yes. You can paint my porch." Casey knocked on the door again after a couple of hours and said,

"I've finished sir, and by the way, your car's not a Porche, it's a BMW."

Stuffed Monkeys

Miss Fortune's only companions were two pet monkeys and when they died she consulted a taxidermist about having them stuffed and preserved. The taxidermist said,

"How would you like them mounted?" And Miss Fortune said, "Couldn't they just be holding hands?"

Wendy

Hanratty was in the men's rest room having a pee and he happened to notice that the man standing next to him had a lady's name tattooed on his penis. Hanratty said,

"Excuse me, but I couldn't help noticing you have 'Wendy' tattooed on your penis. I've got my girlfriend's name tattooed on my penis and her name happens to be Wendy also." And the man said,

"Ah no man. Mine says, 'Welcome To Jamaica And Have A Nice Day."

> *"My parents were in the iron and steel business. My mother did the ironing, and my father went out stealing."*

Good Friday

It was Good Friday and Mrs. Shananegin came out of church with a very pious look on her face, went into the delicatessen, and said to the new young assistant,

"I'll have four ounces of that smoked salmon you've got in the window."

"But that's not smoked salmon," the new assistant said, "that's ham."

"Did I ask you for an opinion?" she said crossly.

Irish Whiskey Cake

Ingredients:
3 bottles of Irish whiskey.
8 oz. of mixed dried fruit.
4 oz. butter.
4 oz. soft brown sugar.
2 large eggs
8 oz. plain flour.
1 tsp. of mixed spice.
1 tsp. of baking powder.

Method:
Open one of the bottles of whiskey. Take a few swigs to see if it's genuine Irish and 70% proof. Cream the butter and sugar. Check the quality of the whiskey again by drinking one full measure. Then add the flesh leggs one at a time and clend to a bleamy consistency. Allow sixture to mettle for a mew finutes while you dour and prink another mull feasure of whiskey. Trinkle in the flour, the baking powder and the sibed vice. Add the dixed mried fruit. Wix mell. Tip tin into cake an bake at 350 for one hour. Make holes in cop of take. Open second bottle of whiskey. Sip slowly while waiting for cool to cake. When cake stops moving, pour any re-

maining whiskey in holes. Hash Wands. Open third bottle of whiskey. Invite friends over. Share the chiskey and wake and they'll soon be saying. "Whoopee! That's the best whiskey take I've ever casted."

Skinner, Tupper and Dupper

An American raised his glass and said to his British friend,

"Here's to Skinner who took his best girl out to dinner. At half past nine it was in her, the dinner, not Skinner. He was in her 'fore dinner."

A few days later, the Brit said to one of his friends,

"I heard an interesting toast the other day which goes: 'Here's to Tupper who took his best girl out to supper. At half past nine it was up her, not Dupper and not the supper, but some son-of-a-bitch named Skinner."

Fuke It

The CEO of a company making detergents and washing powders called an urgent meeting with department heads.

"I've got bad news," he said, "we've failed to maintain our market share and unless we can come up with something new and quite spectacular by the end of the year the whole firm could go belly up." The first to speak was the head of the advertising department who said, "The product's great. What I think's wrong is the name. I think we should repackage it and rename our product 'Fuke.'"

"Fuke? Fuke? " exclaimed the CEO, "What a funny name."

"I can see it now on TV," the advertising manager

went on, "and the jingle goes like this - *If Tide Doesn't Whiten It - And Cheer Doesn't Brighten It - Fuke It.*"

The Flying Doctor

Two guys were prospecting in the Australian outback. One guy went behind a bush to relieve himself and was bitten by a snake. He rushed out and told his friend that a rattlesnake had bitten him on his penis. He begged his friend to do something. The friend told him that the nearest telephone was about 4 miles away and that he would run all the way and contact the flying doctor. He ran the 4 miles in a minute and a half, and spoke to the flying doctor. The flying doctor said he was 300 miles away, and couldn't get there in time with the snake bite antidote.

"Your friend will die within 30 minutes," he said, "so

"Finbarr? I'm in the loo. I have your lousy literary review before me. Soon it will be behind me."

the only thing to do is is run back, take your pocket knife and make a small incision next to the bite, and then suck the poison out."

He thanked the doctor, and ran all the way back. But this time his friend's penis has swollen to about six times the normal size and he was obviously very weak and in great pain.

"When will the doc get here and what did he say?" he managed to gasp. And his friend replied,

"Doc's not coming mate, and he says you're gonna die."

Father O'Flynn's Slippers

The Mother Superior in charge of the hospital nursing sisters was doing her rounds one morning and everyone she met smiled at her and wished her a good morning. When she got back to her office she said to her assistant,

"Can you tell me Sister Immaculata, why everyone is smiling and being so nice to me this morning?"

"It must be because you got out of bed on the wrong side this morning, Reverend Mother."

"Now that you mention it, I did," the Reverend Mother said, "But how did you know that?" Sister Immaculata smiled and said,

"Because you're wearing Father O'Flynn's slippers."

"Midas had a solid gold one."

A Good Sport

An Australian named Digger and his girlfriend were walking past a billabong when she turned to him and said, "I'm pregnant, and I want you to know that if you don't marry me, I'll drown myself in this billabong." And Digger said, "Gee Sheila, not only are you a good screw, but you're a bloody good sport as well."

Ho! Ho !Ho!

Santa came down the chimney one Christmas Eve and a beautiful girl with an hourglass figure came into the room and said,

"Santa I'm a bit lonely tonight, won't you please stay and play?"

Santa said, "Ho! Ho! Ho! Hey! Hey! Hey! Gotta go. Lots of things to do tonight you know." So she took off her dress, smiled seductively at Santa and said,

"Santa don't you want to party just a little with me?" Santa said, "Ho! Ho! Ho! Hey! Hey! Hey! Gotta go. Lots of things to do tonight you know." The girl then took off all her clothes and she was gorgeous. She reached out and put both of her arms around Santa's neck, pressed her naked body close to his and said,

"Santa please stay. Won't you let me ring your ding-a-ling-ling this way"?

"Ho! Ho! Ho! Hey! Hey! Hey!" Santa said, "Gotta stay. Can't get back up the chimney this way."

Shakespeare's 5 Plays

Mr. Flim of Flim, Flam, Adcon and Bamboozle asked Murphy if he could create a book cover design for a publisher who was about to publish a book containing just 5 of Shakespeare's plays. Murphy's design showed

5 boxes. The first box said "Wet". The second "Dry". The third said "3". The fourth said "6" and the fifth said "9".

"Interesting enough I suppose," Mr.Flim said, "but what's this got to do with the 5 Shakespearian plays?"

"I had hoped it was obvious," Murphy said.

"Wet represents 'A Midsummer Night's Dream.' Dry represents 'Love's Labour Lost.' 3" represents 'Much Ado About Nothing.' 6" represents 'As You Like It' and 9" represents 'The Taming Of The Shrew.'"

The Widow And The Sexy Gorilla

There were these two elderly, but still very attractive widows who had been friends for years. Each lived on the opposite side of a dense African jungle. One day a large male gorilla in heat, came out of the jungle, broke into the home of one of the widows, found her nude in the shower and without more ado, forced himself on her. The news of the attack spread quickly and it wasn't long before the other widow at the opposite side of the jungle heard about it. But she didn't visit her friend for six months, thinking that by then her friend would perhaps have recovered enough to talk about her ordeal.

"I suppose you must still be feeling pretty awful?" she consolingly said to her friend. The other widow sounded very dejected as she replied,

"Yes, I still feel pretty awful but what upsets me most of all is that he don't call me. He don't send me flowers....."

"When I told my friend I was having an affair, she said. "Who's doing the catering?"

Molested Twice

Two good-looking nuns were passing an isolated building site when a couple of laborers grabbed them, pushed them into the tool shed and molested them. As they were leaving the one nun turned to the other and said,

"What do you think Mother Superior will say when we tell her we've been molested twice?" And the other nun said,

"But we were only molested once!"

"I know," was the reply, "but we're coming back this way again today, aren't we?"

Suntanned All Over

Hardman O'Houligan was looking at his naked body in the bathroom mirror and noticed he was tanned all over except for his penis. So he went to a deserted beach, took off all his clothes and buried himself in the sand, leaving only his penis sticking up. Two old ladies in their 80's happened to be walking along the beach, and although their eyesight was bad, one of them spotted O'Houligan's penis sticking up out of the sand. She pointed to it with her walking stick and said to her friend,

"It's so sad about sex. When I was 20 I was afraid of it. When I was 30 I couldn't get enough of it. When I was 40 I paid for it. When I was 60 I prayed for it. When I was 70 I'd have died for it. But now that I am 80 and too old to even squat on it, the damn things appear to be growing wild on the beach."

Drunk In The Pulpit

The newly ordained Catholic priest was nervous about his first sermon and he told Father O'Flynn that he felt like he had butterflies in his stomach. Father O'Flynn said that it was hard to get rid of butterflies but that when he was a young priest he had found that a couple of swigs of the communion wine had at least helped him make the butterflies fly in formation. The young priest was so nervous he drank half a bottle of communion wine and when he went into the pulpit he was quite drunk. After mass he said to the old parish priest, "How did I do, father?" Father O'Flynn replied,

"You did very well father, except for three small things. When you want the congregation to give generously, it's best not to call them a bunch of miserable old misers. And as for your stories from the Old Testament,

David slew Goliath. He didn't kick his ass all over the field. And finally, Delilah cut off Samson's hair, not his balls."

Graffiti On A Tipperary Tombstone

A Tipperary man lost his wife and erected a large headstone on her grave, engraved with this message "*The Light Of My Life Has Gone Out.*" However he soon began to fancy another lady and married her within six months. A local wit then scrawled these words on the headstone: "*He struck another match.*"

Sex On Sundays

A very devout Catholic went to see Father O'Flynn and said, "Tell me Father, is it a sin if I have sex with my wife just before or after Mass on Sundays and Holy Days of Obligation?" Father O'Flynn pondered the complexities of the question for a long time and finally said, "No. It's not a sin, provided you don't take pleasure in it."

The Blind Man And The Stray Dog

A blind man was slowly tap-tapping his way along Bachelor's Walk by the side of the Liffey river, in Dublin. When he reached the busy intersection at O'Connell Bridge, he stood waiting with the rest of the pedestrians for the lights to change.

As he was standing there a stray dog wandered up, cocked its leg and peed all over his shoes and his trouser leg. Realizing what had happened, the blind man felt in his pocket, pulled out a small candy bar, and stooping down with the candy bar in his hand, he called the dog.

"Good dog," he said, "Nice, nice doggie. Come here boy."

A man who was also waiting to cross the street touched the blind man and said,

"Excuse me sir. I watched that big Labrador pee all over your shoes and up your trousers leg. Then I see you offering the dog a candy bar. What an extraordinarily kind thing do. You must really love dogs."

"Not really," replied the blind man, "I'm trying to find out where the son-of-a-bitches head is, so I can kick his ass."

Fresh Air

Mrs. O'Nions went to Dr. O'Flannel complaining about flatulence.

"Have you been eating anything unusual?" the doctor asked.

"I have been eating Brussels sprouts, tinned beans, onions and garlic," she said.

"Excuse me," said the doctor. "I'll be back in just a few moments," and he hurriedly left the consulting room. When he came back he was carrying a long wooden pole

with a metal hook at the end. Somewhat alarmed, Mrs O'Nions anxiously said,

"What in the name of God are you thinking of doing with that pole, doctor?"

"Don't worry Mrs. O'Nions," Dr. O'Flannel assured her, "I'm only going to use it to open a window in here."

The Randy Old Goat

Shorty after she was 50, Biddy Mulligan began to put on a lot of weight around the middle, so she went to see Dr. O'Flannel.

"It's absolutely amazing at your age," the docter said, "but you're about 4 months pregnant, Mrs. Mulligan!"

"That's terrible news, doctor" she replied. "I'm now nearly 51 and my husband Moriarty is nearly 65. Could I use your phone? I'd like to speak to the randy old goat

right now and tell him what I think of him." When she got through she said,

"Moriarty you are a selfish, careless pig. You've gone and got me pregnant." There was a long silence at the other end of the telephone, and eventually Moriarty said, "Who is this speaking please?"

The Doctor's Wife

Doctor O'Flannel was having a terrible row with his wife one morning before he left for the hospital.

"You're a lousy house-keeper," he told her. "You're a rotten cook. You're a poor mother, and in bed, you're about as passionate as a plate of cold porridge." That afternoon he returned from the hospital a little earlier than usual, and found his wife in bed with another doctor.

"What the hell's going on here?" he roared. And she said, "I just thought I'd get a second opinion dear."

Mountains Out Of Molehills

A lady who was rather flat-chested heard about Dr. O'Flannel's reputation as someone who could make mountains out of molehills. So she went to see him and he advised her to practice crossing her arms as often as possible while chanting,

"Mary had a little lamb whose fleece was white as snow. And if I keep on doing this, my bust is sure to grow." She was walking in the park one day and seeing no one about started doing her chest exercise.

"Mary had a little lamb whose fleece was white as snow. And if I keep on doing this my bust is sure to grow." Suddenly she spotted a man watching her intently from a park bench. He smiled and said,

"I can tell you've been to see the famous body recontouring expert, Dr.O'Flannel."

"Yes. But how did you know?" she said, somewhat amazed.The man stood up, jumped up and down and said, "Hickory, Dickory, Dock...."

Timbuctoo

Casey and Murphy applied to join the Dublin Literary Society but were told by the secretary that only one new member could be accepted at that particular time. The secretary invited each of them to make up a short poem using the word Timbuctoo; and advised them that the winner would be eligible for immediate membership.

Casey said, "*I walked along a distant shore. I spied a maiden in a door. Her hair was gold. Her eyes were blue. I knew I was in Timbuctoo.*"

And Murphy said, "*It was to a far off-land we went, my friend Tim and I. We spied three maidens in a tent, Tim and I. They swore they would love us, and always be true. But they were three, and we were too, So I bucked one, and Tim bucked two.*"

Religious Views

Two young men wearing navy blue suits and carrying The Book of Mormon, knocked on Mrs. Shananegin's front door and said, "Mornin' m'am. We're from the Mormon Church. We were wondering whether you have any particular religious views?"

"I wouldn't go so far as to call them religious views," Mrs. Shananegin said, "but I do have a couple of snaps of me and Seamus taken outside the Vatican last summer."

The Two Bitches

An American travelling in Ireland got on a crowded train. There was only one empty seat but before he could sit down, a lady lifted her poodle off the floor and sat it on the seat. The American politely asked her if she would mind removing her dog.

"No" she snarled abruptly.

Without saying a word the American slid down the glass panel in the door of the carriage, picked up the dog and slung it out the window. Before the dumbfounded dog owner could say a word, another gentleman leaned across and said to the American,

"Pardon my intrusion, sir" he said "but you Yanks have got it all wrong. You drive on the wrong side of the road. You eat with the fork in your right hand - and now you have just thrown the wrong bitch off the train."

The Lottery Winner

A telegram arrived addressed to Mrs. Mulligan. She read it slowly three times. She did some chores and went upstairs to the bedroom, and awoke her sleeping husband.

"I've just won a million in the lottery," she said. "I've been up for three hours and I've already got my bags packed. Get up now, Moriarty. I want you to have all your bags packed and be ready to leave the house within an hour."

"Wonderful news, darling," Mulligan said, "Where are we going?"

"I am leaving on an-around-the-world cruise alone," she said. "You just pack your bags, Moriarty, and be out of the house within an hour."

Bromide In The Tea

Fergal and Finbarr, two 80 year-old men who had been friends for years, were sitting on a bench in Dublin's Phoenix Park, when Fergal suddenly turned to Finbarr.

"There's a funny thing," he said, "You remember that bromide they put in our tea during the first world war?"

"Yes," Finbarr said, "I remember. What of it?"

"I think it's just starting to wear off because I've suddenly got this urge to make love to a woman again."

"What kind of a woman do you fancy?"

Fergal slowly raised his hand and touched the sides of his head. Then he touched his cheek. Then he cupped his hands and held them up in front of his chest.

"I can understand why you might want an intelligent woman," Finbarr said, touching his own temple, "and I can understand why you would want a pretty woman," he said, touching his own cheek, and holding up his own hands, said, "but why you would want one with arthritis in her hands?"

The KGB in Ireland

The KGB sent one of their agents on a secret mission to Ireland. His instructions were to make contact with his Irish counterpart, named Murphy. The secret password to be used by the Russian was, "In Dublin's fair city," and Murphy was supposed to answer, "Where the girls are so pretty." The Russian arrived on an Aeroflot jet and landed at Shannon International Airport. He walked all the way to the coast and was wandering down a narrow country road when he met the local mailman.

"You vill help me?" he said. "I look Meester Murphy?"

"There's quite a few Murphys around here," the mailman replied. "There's Stout Murphy who keeps the 'Wet Your Whistle Pub'. There's Murphy the Milk, and there's

Mad Mike Murphy. And as luck should have it, me own name happens to be Murphy too. Which wan of us will ye be after wantin' now?"

"In Dublin's fair city......" the Russian said. replied,

"It's Murphy The Spy, you want," the mailman said.

A Second Chance

Young Kathleen told her mother she was pregnant.

"And who did it to you, my child?" anxiously enquired the mother.

"It was Marvin Goldburger's youngest son," she said.

"Ah but he's such a nice Jewish boy. Thank God it wasn't some auld go-the-road without as much as two brass farthings to scratch his ass with. Goldburger own three gown shops and he's rolling in money. I'll go and see him and enquire about damages and compensation as marriage between a Jew and a Catholic is out of the question." So she went along and saw the boy's father.

"Mr Goldburger," she said, "your young son has been having nookie with my virgin daughter Kathleen and she's about three months pregnant. We are good Catholics so let's not talk about abortion. As orthodox Jews, I know you can't have your only son David married to a Catholic. So tell me, what do you propose?"

"Don't worry," Goldburger said, "Money is no problem. Your Kathleen will never want for nothing. I'll pay all her expenses. If she has a goy I'll send him to college. If his head should happen to be screwed on the right way, I'll consider taking him into the business with me. If Kathleen should have a shikseh, I'll send her to the best convent school in Dublin, and when it's time for her to marry,I promise you she'shall have a fine dowry."

"Asha the blessings of God on you Mr. Goldburger, but God between ourselves and all harm, what if my Kathleen should be so unlucky as to have a miscarriage, would you and your son be willing to give her a second chance?"

Budweiser Beer

An enterprising young American salesman was sent over to Dublin by the export director of Budweiser Beer. He was instructed to approach the Archbishop of Dublin with a very lucrative offer.

"Here's the deal, your Grace," he said. "In return for you instructing all your parish priests to change just one word in The Lord's Prayer, I am authorized to offer you the sum of one million dollars."

"A million dollars?" the Archbishop said in amazement, "Do you mean Budweiser will actually give the Catholic Church in Ireland one million dollars just for changing one word? What word?"

"When your priests are speaking from the pulpit on Sundays," replied the beer salesman, "instead of saying 'Give us this day our daily bread', Budweiser Beers want them to say, 'Give us this day our daily Bud.'"

"We sure could do with the money for the new schools and all," the Archbishop said, "but it's more than my job's worth to change a single word in our Lord's own Prayer. But I will personally go to Rome immediately and consult a higher authority." He took an Aer Lingus flight to the Holy City and was given an audience with a couple of high-placed Cardinals in the Vatican. He explained the deal and said,

"You must agree it is a very, very tempting offer?"

"Si. It is a lotta money," one of the Cardinals agreed. Then turning towards his colleague, he said,

"Paulo, whena does our contract with Wonder Bread expire?"

A Good Port

A English visitor went into Neary's Bar in Dublin and ordered a plate of smoked salmon, brown whole meal soda bread, Kerrygold butter and a couple of wedges of lemon.

"An what'll ye have to drink sir?" the barman asked.

"Your food is very good," replied the Englishman," and you can get a decent cup of tea or coffee in Bewley's Cafe in Grafton Street. But I've been over here for the last three weeks and I've yet to find a decent drink. I've tried your beer and it tastes like cat's pee. I've tried your black porter and it's like dirty bog water. I've tried your whiskey and it's as weak as a wet noodle. Can you possibly recommend a good port?"

"Aye that I can," the barman replied. "The Port of Dun

Laoghaire....and if you hurry yourself sir, ye'll be able to catch the afternoon boat back to where ever the hell ye came from."

The Killer Dog

A tourist motoring in Ireland came to a little village and was obliged to stop to allow a funeral procession to pass. He noticed that there were only men in the procession, and that the man walking immediately behind the hearse was holding a steel chain with a large Irish Wolfhound attached to the other end.

"Who's dead?" enquired the tourist.

"Do you see that man behind the coffin with the big dog? It's his wife that's dead," he replied.

"How did she die?" the tourist enquired. And the local man said,

"Himself with the dog likes a drop or two of the hard

stuff and he'd been out having a few jars with the lads when he came home a bit late one night last week, and his wife started giving him hell. Then she hit him over the head with his own blackthorn stick. Then his auld dog, which was lying there sleeping by the turf fire, jumped up on top of her, and before you could even say Paddy McGinty's Goat, he'd bit a lump as big as a black pudding out of her throat and killed her stone dead."

"I am sorry to hear that," said the tourist, "but I wonder if he would consider selling the dog?"

"Aye. To be sure the auld dog's for sale right enough," said the mourner. "but there's a waiting list. You'll have to get in the queue with the rest of us."

Nigel's 12 Christmas Gifts

The First Day of Christmas

My Darling Nigel,
I never thought I would hear from you again after our divorce. I was surprised to receive your totally unexpected gift out of the blue. The partridge is really cute and I just love the pear tree. Happy holidays. Warmly and still quite affectionately yours,
Fiona.

The Second Day of Christmas

My Dearest Nigel, You Are Such A Sweetie,
Thanks for your surprise gift of two turtle doves. They are just darling. I guess I misjudged you when I once called you a mean old fart. Your kindness overwhelms me.
Ever yours,
Fiona.

The Third Day of Christmas

Dearest Nigel Pet,
Thank you for yet another absolutely amazing Christmas gift. Three French hens! I can't think what's come over you lately? What's with you and all these birds? I just want you to know that the French hens were quite vicious. They killed the turtle doves and then ate them. Could they have possibly been vultures? The poor partridge saw this cannibalistic massacre happen and promptly died of fright, and Nigel, I'm not feeling too good myself. Enough is enough already. Don't send any more frigging birds.
      Your Ex-wife   Fiona

The Fourth Day of Christmas

Nigel, you son-of-a-bitch,
When I opened the door this morning there were 4 calling birds on the doorstep. I have to tell you I am getting just a little bit pissed off with all these frigging birds. You know how house-proud I am. All those loose feathers and bird droppings really get up my nose. I never want to see you or another bird again.
      Fiona

The Fifth Day of Christmas

Nigel honey,
Your thoughtful gift of 5 golden rings arrived this morning. You certainly know how to sweet-talk a girl when you want to, and just when I was beginning to suspect a foul plot? Please forgive me. Do the rings have some special message? Are you trying to tell me something in a subtle way?
      Fiona

The Sixth Day of Christmas

Nigel, you stinking foul pest,

Just when I thought there was a chance we could at least be friends again, your special delivery messenger arrived and left me with six cackling geese. They are laying broken eggs all over my best Persian rug. You make me sick, sick, sick.

Fiona

The Seventh Day of Christmas

Nigel, you are a frigging nerd,

Just what the hell do you think you are playing at? There are now seven swans a-swimming in the lily pond. What's with you and all those frigging birds? I am walking about in bird shit up to my ankles. I am a complete nervous wreck and I can't sleep. Please lay off sending me any more of those awful shitty birds.

Fiona.

The Eighth Day of Christmas

Nigel, you jerk,

What the hell am I going to do with 8 maids a-milking and their shitty cows? The whole of the front lawn is covered with cow shit and the smell is shocking. The geese have stopped laying. The swans got so disgusted they flew away. As for the 3 French hens, they ate something nasty and immediately rolled over on their backs in the front room and died twitching horribly. Why are you doing all these terrible things to me? Why? Why? Why?

Fiona.

The Ninth Day of Christmas

OK smart-ass, up yours too,
When I opened the door this morning, nine fat, old dancing ladies waltzed in. They were made up like painted Jezebels and looked like they escaped from some geriatric whore-house. Their grab-a-granny dance costumes were very scanty. Just four little bunches of feathers, yes feathers, a suspender belt, black fishnet stockings and black shoes with stiletto heels. They have ruined the polished parquet floor and you, you animal, have ruined my Christmas. Mother was right. If only I had believed her when she said you only married me for my money. I'm warning you buster, just don't make me any madder than I am right now, or God knows what I might do.

Fiona.

The Tenth Day of Christmas

Nigel, you dirty rotten swine,
This time you have gone too far. Ten lords came-a-leaping around my once-lovely living room. They soon spotted the milking maids, leaped on top of them and actually started bonking them. And you know how much I hate that sort of thing. I have reported their extraordinarily lewd and lascivious behavior to The National League of Decency. Their cavorting and carrying on has even frightened the cows and has caused them to stampede madly all over the house. The noise is awful and the neighbors have got so tired of politely complaining that they are now threatening to have me evicted. You are an incredibly cruel, cold hearted wicked bastard, and I'll never forgive you.
Fiona.

The Eleventh Day of Christmas

Nigel, you rotten shithead bastard,

Eleven pipers paraded up the driveway this morning and I'll swear every Goddamn one of them was playing a different tune. My migraine is killing me, I think I am about to have another nervous breakdown. You have finally pushed me too far and in order to preserve what's left of my sanity, I am instructing my attorneys, Froggins and Bloggins to apply for a writ prohibiting you from ever harassing and tormenting me again.

Fiona.

The Twelfth Day of Christmas

Nigel, you have really pissed me off this time,

Twelve drummers drumming on their frigging drums came to torment me this morning. I tried to stop them getting in but they broke the door down and joined the rest of the mad menagerie.

The six geese were trampled to death when the cows stampeded. My once-lovely house is now completely ruined. It's a horrible stinking mess of cow manure, dead animals, sweaty bodies, feathers and bird shit. The police, fire brigade and an ambulance have arrived and I think they are going to take me away. I think I am going quite mad. I need help. I don't seem to be able to cope on my own any longer. You have finally succeeded in pushing me over the top.

Fiona.

--- ♣ ---

Froggins and Bloggins
Attorneys at Law,
Suite #14, Plaza Tower Buildings, Newtown.

Dear Sir,

International Cablegram
This is to formally acknowledge the twelve Christmas gifts which you have seen fit to use as a means of fiendishly torturing our client, Ms.Fiona Fothergill. It is our duty to inform you that we are instituting legal proceedings against you and we shall be looking for very substantial damages, not only to the real estate but also in respect of the mental anguish and pain and suffering you have callously inflicted upon our client, who is now, we are sad to say, an inmate of Our Lady Of Perpetual Sorrows Convent Sanitarium.

Yours faithfully,
Froggins and Bloggins.

The Lion's Share
Back in the days when Britannia ruled the waves, an English navy captain decided to become a pirate and advertised discreetly for a couple of money-motivated partners. An Irishman and a Scotsman applied and were

taken on. They had a very successful season and when it was time to divide the bounty, the English captain ordered the Scotsman to divide it into 3 portions. The Scotsman divided the bounty fairly and squarely into 3 equal portions. On seeing this, the English captain became extremely annoyed and drawing his cutlass, took a swipe at the Scotsman and cut off his head. The captain then turned to the Irishman and said, "Patrick, now you divide the loot." So the Irishman proceeded to make 2 piles, one very small and one very large, and indicated that the lion's share belonged to the captain. Then the captain said "Who taught you to count so good?"' And Patrick said, "You did."

An Act of Faith

Two nuns were driving along a country road when they ran out of gas. The nearest garage was over a mile away. They didn't have a can but they did have a chamber pot which they always kept hidden under the back seat.

"We'll both walk back to the nearest gas station," the one said, "and we'll get a gallon of gas in the chamber pot." So they carried the chamber pot filled with gas back to the car. They made a funnel out of a copy of 'The Catholic Messenger' and were pouring in the gas when a well known Protestant minister, who was driving by, stopped his car, opened the window and said,

"Good afternoon ladies. You well know I don't like your Pope, nor your religion, but I do admire your faith."

The Two Sparrows

There were the two sparrows, a male and a female, and they lived in different parts of the town. They arranged to meet at a certain spot at a certain time. It was a lovely

---
🍀
---

day. The sun was shining. The bees were humming and all the birds were twittering, so the boy sparrow decided to walk rather than fly. As a result, he was an hour late for his date. The girl sparrow wasn't there, and he wondered if she'd left thinking she'd been stood up? But he decided to hang around for a bit and in a little while the girl sparrow arrived, looking very bruised and battered and with half her feathers missing.

"What ever happened to you?" he said. And she said,

"On my way here I flew over the park. I saw a crowd of people gathered around a couple wearing shorts, and playing some kind of game. I flew down to have a closer look, and before I knew what was happening, I got caught up in a game of badminton."

A Fat One Or A Thin One?

Pat said to his friend Mike, "What kind of woman do you like?"

"What do you mean?" Mike replied.

"I mean do you like a fat one or a thin one?" Pat asked.

"A thin one," Mike admitted.

"Do you like a young one or an old one?" Pat said.

"A young one," replied Mike.

"Do you like a pretty one or an ugly one?" Pat said.

"A pretty one, of course," replied Mike.

"Then," said Pat, "why the hell are you messing with my wife?"

A Short Distance

When I was in Dublin I asked a passer-by how far it was to the nearest Taxi station. "It's only a five minutes walk," he said, "if you run all the way."

The Three Legged-Chicken

A motorist was doing 70 miles an hour down the Naas Road dual carriageway outside Dublin when to his amazement he was overtaken by a three-legged chicken doing about 80 miles an hour. He chased after the chicken nearly all the way to Kildare when it suddenly cut across in front of him, turned into a driveway, and disappeared around the back of a large Georgian farmhouse. The astonished motorist knocked at the farmhouse door and said,

"Pardon me, but I've just been overtaken by a three-legged chicken doing about 80 miles an hour and it ran in here and around the back of your house."

"Yes," said the farmer, "I breed three-legged chickens and there's a whole flock of them running wild out there in my back paddock."

"Aren't three-legged chickens who can do 80 miles an hour just little bit unusual?" enquired the motorist.

"I have a degree in genetic engineering," the farmer said, "and there's me, there's my missus and there's our son Brian. Every time we had a chicken for dinner, we were always fighting amongst ourselves over who should get a drumstick. So I thought it would save all the arguments at meal times if I were to breed three-legged chickens."

"What do they taste like?" the astonished motorist asked.

"I'm afraid I don't know," replied the farmer. "We haven't managed to catch one yet."

The Naughty Nun

A bunch of nuns were walking along the beach at Brittas Bay, County Wicklow, and one young novice nun got lost in the sand dunes. When the rest of the nuns eventually found her she was looking a bit the worse for wear.

"Whatever happened to you, Sister Mary Josephine?" they said.

"I was picking up sea shells and when I looked up, you were all gone. Then I met this young man. He said I was far too pretty to waste myself on being a nun. Then he held my hand and started kissing and fondling me, and, I think he might have had sex with me?"

"When we get back to the convent," the Mother Superior said sternly, "I want to have a very serious talk with you in my study." After delivering a stern lecture, the Mother Superior said,

"Go into the pantry now child, and you'll find a bowl of fruit. Pick the biggest lemon you can find, cut it in two and then suck on both halves as hard as you possibly can."

"And will that stop me getting pregnant, Reverend Mother?" enquired the now very anxious Mary Josephine.

"No," replied the Mother Superior, "but it might help to wipe that stupid smile off your face".

Mick McGoolie And The Sperm Bank

Mick McGoolie regularly donated a pint of his blood to the blood bank. On this particular occasion he saw a sign which said 'Sperm Bank' and another one that said 'Blood Bank'.

"If it's all the same to you," he said to the nurse, "this time I think I would like to donate some sperm." The nurse gave him a screw-top jar and ushered him into a private cubicle. An hour and a half went by and he was still in there. The nurse and waiting donors could hear

a lot of moaning and groaning and loud banging noises coming from the cubicle. Eventually the nurse bravely knocked on the cubicle door and shouted,

"Are you alright in there Mr. McGoolie?"

"No, I'm not," he said, "I've pulled it and I've twisted it. I've used my left hand and then my right hand, and I've even tried banging it on the table, but I still can't get the lid off the screw-top jar."

The Jealous Husband's Heart Attack

These three men died and were being questioned by St. Peter.

"How did you die, Number One?" St. Peter asked.

"I died of a heart attack," he said. "For years I suspected that my wife had been unfaithful. But I had no proof, and was never able to catch her at it. One day I decided to

come home early from the office. I let myself into our seventeenth floor penthouse apartment very quietly. It was about five o'clock in the afternoon and I found her naked in bed. But there was no man about. But I knew she had been entertaining someone, because there were two glasses by the side of the bed, a half a bottle of Jack Daniels and the remains of a magnificent Upmann Havana cigar still burning in the ashtray. She denied everything of course, but I got mad as hell and the more she denied it the madder and madder I became. I charged about the apartment looking for the bastard. I tipped the king-size bed up on end. I ripped the doors off the wardrobe. I tore down all the drapes and I still couldn't find him. In the end I got so mad I picked up the big fridge and slung it through the kitchen window. That was when I got the pain in my chest and had a massive coronary from which I never recovered."

"And how did you die number two?" said St Peter.

"I had only just retired," Number Two said. "I moved down from New Jersey to Florida for the better weather. I bought this beautiful ground floor Condo apartment and was relaxing on the patio by the swimming pool and enjoying my Happy Hour drink when I heard some shouting going on followed by this terrible sound of breaking glass. I looked up and caught a glimpse of this flying fridge just before it landed on my head and killed me." And Number Three said,

"I was hiding inside this fridge when...."

The Hooker

This young virgin boy left home and rented a room in Rathmines, Dublin. One night after he had a few jars in the local pub, he was solicited by a hooker and took her back to his apartment. She insisted on switching off all the lights. They both took off their clothes and got into the bed. He reached out to touch her and suddenly said,

"What kind of woman are you? You've got no bust? You've got no belly button and you've even got no knee caps?"

"Turn me over, dummy," the hooker said.

As Broke As The Ten Commandments

Goldburger came home looking very dejected and said to his wife,

"I have some bad news. The creditors are hounding me. The bank is on my back and I must have a thousand dollars by three o'clock tomorrow. I tried all my friends and they say they are like me, as broke as the Ten Commandments. Vat can ve do?"

"I can let you have a thousand dollars, Marvin," she said.

"Where you get this kind of money from, Beccy?"

"Every time you made love to me" she said "I put a dollar in the cookie jar under the bed."

"Oy, yoi, yoi," Goldburger said, "If only I had known, I would have give you all my business."

The Unhappy Hooker

This middle aged married couple were having difficulty paying the mortgage after the husband was laid-off, and found it impossible to get another job,

"I hate to have to ask you to do this," the husband said to his wife, "but since I can't earn any money, maybe you would consider doing a little bit of soliciting on the street outside the pub?" Even though she had no previous experience of that sort of thing, and didn't think much of the idea anyway, she reluctantly agreed to give it a go.

When she came home in the early hours of the morning after a hard nights work, she and her husband counted the takings, which amounted to $35.00 and 50 cents.

"That's not a lot," complained her husband, "but who was the cheapskate who only gave you the odd 50 cents?"

"Why all of them did."

An Attempt To Bribe The Pope

The Vatican roof was in need of some repairs, and the Pope placed a big advertisement in the "Corriere Della Sera" newspaper, inviting bids. Three contractors submitted estimates. There was an Irish contractor, an Italian contractor and a Jewish contractor. The Irish contractor was the first one to call on the Pope and his estimate was 12 million lira.

"Pat," the Pope said, "The price sounds right and I'd like to give you the job, but you will appreciate it's not my money I'll be spending, and I have to account for all expenditures to the Cardinals. Can you give me a price breakdown in case they ask me some awkward questions?"

"That's easy your Holiness," Pat said, "There's 4 million lira in there for the tiles. There's 4 million labor charges. That leaves just 4 million to cover overheads plus a small margin of profit." The Pope promised to let him know after he had obtained the other two estimates. The Italian contractor submitted the next bid and it was for 24 million lire.

"How did you arrive at your figures Mario?" asked the Pope.

"I only use the very best quality tiles," Mario replied,

"and they are going to cost 8 million lira. Since I refuse to employ unskilled people, the labor charge for my properly licensed and bonded master-craftsmen is 8 million. The remaining 8 million is gross profit. You lika da price?"

"It does seem a bit-top heavy, Mario," replied the Pope, "but I'll let you know." Finally the Pope met the Jewish contractor, Morris Koffcandy. Looking at his business card, which was expensively embossed in gold leaf, The Pope saw that Morry had an MBA degree from Harvard.

"Now Morris," the Pope said, "there's only three of you in the running. There's this Irish fellah, Patrick Casey who has quoted a very very good price of only 12 million lira. Then there's a quote from a local firm Mario De Napoli SA. His bid is 24 million lira. So, now you know what the competition have bid, if you want the job, you'll have to sharpen your pencil quite a bit." Morris smiled but instead of pulling out his pencil, he pulled out two Monte Christo cigars and gave one to the Pope. Then he opened his briefcase, took out a bottle of Dom Perignon champagne and two crystal goblets. He carefully poured the wine, offered the Pope a glass and a cigar, slowly lit his own cigar, took a few puffs and finally said,

"Have I got a deal for you,Your Holiness. I have seen some of Pat Casey's work. I've seen some of Mario De Napoli's work, and I have to say that both of them do a reasonably good job. I can tell you right now without even as much as looking at the roof, that the price you are going to accept is 36 million lira."

"But, Morris," said the Pope, "How can you possibly justify such a high price?"

"Oh that's easy," Morris said, "There's 12 million net profit for me. And there's another 12 million cash in your hand for you. Then we let Pat Casey do the work for 12 million."

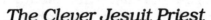

The Clever Jesuit Priest

Kathleen went to confession and said, "Father, I'm in danger of losing my faith. I did the Stations of the Cross. I've said the Rosary every morning and night for the whole month. I've been putting $10.00 in the collection plate every Sunday. I've also lit three dozen holy candles, and even though I've begged and prayed to God on my knees until they were nearly dropping off me, God has refused to answer my prayers or given me the hint of a sign that he's even been listening to me."

"Oh, He heard you alright my child," said the priest, "but maybe it was yourself who wasn't listening when He said `NO."

A Guaranteed Win at the Curragh

Just before the start of the Grand National race on The Curragh at Kildare, the chief steward, on seeing one of the

trainers slip something into his horse's mouth, immediately approached the trainer and enquired if he was attempting to nobble the horse.

"Certainly not," replied the trainer,"I was only giving him 3 lumps of sugar. I've already given him one and here are the other two. To prove they are absolutely harmless, you eat one lump and I'll eat the other."

After eating a lump each, the chief steward went away apparently satisfied. Then the trainer turned to his jockey and gave him these instructions:

"Pull him back for the first couple of furlongs. Then give him his head, and I guarantee no one will catch up with him, unless it happens to be the chief steward or myself."

Sex Lessons At School

A 7-year-old girl came home from school and said to her mother,

"The nuns talked to us about AIDS and sex at school today mammy."

"I think you are a bit young for that," the mother said, "but what did you learn?"

"It was something to do with not having courses with different people, and buying condos for protection."

Under A Scotsman's Kilt

A couple of cheeky English kids on a day trip over the Scottish border, stopped an elderly gentleman wearing a kilt, and said,

"Excuse me sir, but is there anything worn under your kilt?"

"Let me assure you laddies," he said with a smile, "that nothing at all is worn under my kilt. Everything is in perfect working order."

Father O'Flynn's 3 Sermons

Just before delivering his Sunday homily, Father O'Flynn said, "You have a choice of three sermons today. I have a $1.00 sermon that lasts for an hour. I have a $2.00 sermon that that lasts only 30 minutes, and I have $5.00 sermon that I can run through in less than 3 minutes. The ushers will now pass the collection baskets, and after I've looked at the collection, I'll know which sermon you all want."

The Cat And The Caster Oil

A farmer rang the vet and said,
"My calf has constipation. What shall I give it?"
"Give it a pint of caster oil and I'll ring you tomorrow," said the vet. Next day the vet phoned the farmer and said,
"How's the calf?"
"Calf?" said the farmer, "I said 'c-a-t' Cat.'"
"Oh dear. I thought you said 'calf'" replied the vet, who then anxiously enquired about the poor cat.
"Well," said the farmer, "he and three other cats spent the morning digging trenches. They spent the afternoon covering up, and they spent the evening looking for new territory."

The Irish School Inspector

The school inspector was not at all pleased with the answers he received to questions on general knowledge. He then tried asking questions on biblical knowledge, but the results were equally as bad. He approached the headmaster and complained about the appallingly low standard of education he had found.

"I've been a school inspector in Irish schools for over 20 years," he said, "and I've never come across such a collection of idiots. I asked one boy in the 9th grade if he knew who knocked down the walls of Jericho and the boy said, 'Please sir, it wasn't me, sir.'"

"What was the name of that boy?" the headmaster asked.

"Liam Lynch," the inspector replied. The headmaster said,

"I have known that boy since he was in kindergarten and he has never told a lie. If he says he didn't do it, I believe he didn't do it." Then the school inspector called on the boy's parents and spoke to the mother, telling her how he was rather ashamed that her son Liam didn't know who knocked down the walls of Jericho.

"You'll have to speak to the boy's father," she said. So he spoke to the father and repeated what he had told the mother. Then the father said,

"Maybe my Liam is guilty and maybe he is not. But I don't want any trouble. How much will it cost to rebuild these walls?"

The Thief In The Cinema

Goldburger loved to play the horses but his track record showed that he had picked twice as many losers as winners. On this particular occasion he felt so lucky that he was able to persuade his-long suffering wife, Rebecca, to loan him enough housekeeping money to back his hunch at Leopardstown Races.

"If I win," he promised, "I'll take you out to dinner at the Shelbourne and afterwards I'll let you choose which film you want to go and see."

He placed a 'To Win' bet of $50.00 and his horse came in at five to one. First they had a few happy hour drinks and then went in to dinner. Before going on to the cinema, Goldburger gave Rebecca what was left of his winnings to mind. Not having a handbag or purse with her on this occasion, she decided the safest place for the money was up inside the tight elastic legs of her old-fashioned panties. When they got home Goldburger said "Gimme the money Beccy. I want to count how much we have left." She felt inside her panties but the money wasn't there.

"The gelt's all gone," she screamed. "I've been robbed. It must have been that man who was sitting next to me in the cinema. He must have stolen the money when he put his hand on my leg and inside my panties." Goldburger exploded.

"Do you mean to say you allowed some total stranger to put his hand up the leg of your panties in the dark?

"Yes, but how was I to know he was a thief?" Rebecca said.

The Warden's Ball

A prison official was selling tickets outside Dublin's Mountjoy Prison. He stopped a Dubliner and said,

"Buy a $1.00 ticket for the Prison Warden's Ball, sir?"
"I'll take 10 tickets," the Dubliner said, "and maybe they'll castrate more than one of them?"

Geriatric Golf

A nearly blind elderly golfer wanted to play golf at Malahide Golf Club on the North side of Dublin, and after he had told the club secretary about his physical handicap, the Captain said,

"I'll fix you up with another elderly gentleman I know, but even though he is 85 years old, he has 20 - 20 vision. Together you'll make a great team." The one with the perfect eyesight told his friend where the ball was and after the nearly blind one played the shot, he said,

"Did you see that shot?" And his elderly friend replied,

"Yes. But I forget where the ball went."

Half A Head Of Cabbage

A man went into a greengrocers shop just off Patrick Street, Cork, and said he wanted to buy a half a head of Savoy cabbage. The greengrocer's assistant said that the man would have to purchase a whole head. But the man insisted that he only wanted a half a head. Rather than argue with a man who was over six feet tall and weighed about 350 pounds, the assistant went through to the back of the shop and said to his boss,

"There's a silly old fool out there who is insisting on buying only half a head of cabbage." Just then, out of the corner of his eye, he saw that the man had followed him in and was standing right there beside him, so he immediately added,

"And this fine gentleman wants to buy the other half, sir."

Religious Prejudice

Two old friends met on the flight to Belfast, Northern Ireland, from Heathrow, London. One asked his friend why he was taking the trip. His friend who had a slight stammer, said,

I'm g...going...f...for...a...jo...jo...job as an...an..announcer with the Belfast Broadcasting Company."

"Don't you mean as a technician in the back room?"

"No...no...I..I...mean as an...an...announcer."

When they met again later that evening on the flight back to London, the one said,

"How did you get on at the interview?"

"Sh...sh...sure...a...a...Ca...Ca...Catholic has no chance at all of getting a job in Protestant Belfast."

The Sexy Protestant

Father O'Flynn was going around the men's hospital ward, stopping to say a few kind words at each bedside.

"And how is yourself feeling today?" he said to the first man.

"Fine, Father, just fine. Can't wait to get home to the wife and family."

"How many family have you got?"

"Well, there's the wife and myself and seven children, Father."

"You're a good Catholic I suppose?"

"Aye Father."

"God bless you my son," was the reply. Father O'Flynn carried out similar conversations with the other patients and the average family size was four children. Finally he came to the man in the end bed who said he had seventeen children. The priest asked him what parish he belonged to, and the man replied,

"I'm a Protestant, Father."

"Oh," said Father O'Flynn and quickly backed away from the man's bed. On his way out he met the ward sister and said,

"You'll need to watch that fella in the end bed. He's a bit of a sex maniac."

Pregnancy -The Good And Bad News

A young woman went to see Dr. O'Flannel and complained about her morning sickness.

"Mrs Carriage," the doctor said with a big smile on his face, "the good news is that you are going to have a baby."

"It's MISS Carriage, doctor," she blushingly said.

"In that case, Miss Carriage," Dr. O'Flannel said, "the bad news is that you are pregnant."

Henpecked

St. Peter met a bunch of new recruits outside the Pearly Gates and had them line up for inspection.

"Step forward all those men who were henpecked by their wives when they were on earth," he said.

All the men stepped forward except for one small, rather weedy, wimpy looking man. St. Peter went up to him and said, "OK, macho man, what's your story?"

And the meek little man replied,

"My wife told me never to make a move without first getting her permission."

An "F" In Sex

A young schoolboy asked his grandmother how old she was, and the grandmother said,

"It's just not polite to ask a lady her age."

Later on the boy took a peek at her ID card and said,

"I know how old you are Gran. You're 65 years old. You're 5' 2". You have blue eyes. You have brown hair. You weigh 125 pounds and you got an 'F' in sex."

Choosing A Book Keeper

Casey and Murphy were discussing business over lunch.

"Did you get yourself fixed up with a new book keeper yet?' Murphy asked.

"Yes," replied Casey, "I contacted Girl Power Number Crunchers Agency and they sent me three applicants. When I asked the first one a simple question like how much is two and two, she said `Four'. The second one said, `The answer is Four if you add them up, and Twenty Two if you write them side by side.' But the third one looked at me very shrewdly and said `It depends on whether you are buying or selling'"

"How interesting," observed Murphy, "I am curious as to which one you employed. The first one was obviously very conservative. The second one had great imagination and creativity, but the third one instinctively knew that Two and Two is whatever you want it to be. I suppose you chose her?"

"No," said Casey, "I chose the one with the biggest boobs."

> "Why do you read Playboy and The National Explorer?" "Because I like to look at places I'm never going to get to visit."

The Oldest Ancestor

An Englishman, an Irishman and a Jew were discussing ancestry, and the Englishman proudly boasted,

"One of my ancestors received a Knighthood directly from Richard the Lionheart."

"One of mine received Holy Communion from the hand of Blessed Saint Patrick himself," the Irishman claimed.

And the Jew said, "I can do better than you lot. One of my ancestors, Moses, was the very first man to actually break all of the Ten Commandments at the same time."

The Three Tailors

Three Dublin tailors all of whom had a shop in O'Connell Street, were in fierce competition with each other. In an attempt to outsmart the others and attract more business, one placed a big sign in his shop window announcing that he was 'The Best Tailor in Dublin'. Not wishing to be outsmarted, the second one placed an even bigger sign in his window with the proud boast 'The Best Tailor in Ireland'. The third tailor then put up a modest sized sign that simply proclaimed him to be 'The Best Tailor in This Street!'

Sexy from Sneem

RTE Radio sent an outside broadcasting unit down to the somewhat remote but very picturesque town of Sneem in County Kerry, to follow up a newspaper story that Kerrymen, and Sneem inhabitants in particular, were the sexiest men in all Ireland.

"Could it be the pure mountain water, do you think, that makes Kerrymen so virile?" the reporter asked an elderly villager.

"Dunno," was the reply.

So the reporter asked another question.

"Just how old are you, sir, and how many children do you have in your family?'

"Let me think now," the elderly villager replied, "I'll be sixty next birthday and I have seventeen children. No, better make that eighteen. I nearly forgot that my wife Nuala had another child last week."

"My goodness," exclaimed the reporter, "that must be a record?"

"Well, not exactly," was the reply, "my own father had twenty children."

"Wonderful," said the reporter, "If he was alive I would have liked to have interviewed him."

"Oh he's very much alive and kicking, but he's gone to a wedding over at Cahirciveen," the son said.

"A grandson or grand-daughters wedding would that be?" the reporter enquired.

"Ach no. His own. Me da's still a randy old goat at eighty five."

"Well that's simply incredible," the reporter said, "but why would an eighty five year old man who has already reared a fine big family, and no doubt lived a very full and happy life down here in God's own County, want to get married again at his age?"

"To be perfectly honest with you, sir," was the reply, "he didn't actually want to get married, but the girl's father said if he didn't marry her, he would shoot him."

Dublin's Mary Street Market

Three were elderly women sidewalk fruit sellers, wearing long black shawls over their aprons, loudly proclaiming their wares in piercingly clear sing-song voices, in Dublin's Mary Street Market.

"Granny Smith's. Golden Delicious. All lovely and juicy," the first lady sang.

"The biggest fruit. The best fruit. The cheapest fruit," cried the second lady. Not to be outdone or outsold by the competition, the third one loudly sang,

"Apples without worms! Apples without worms."

Goat Hormone Injections

Clarissa Cassidy had returned to her home after an absence abroad of seven years, and went to visit Dr. O'Flannel, who had been a close friend.

"I hope you don't mind me asking you this Clarissa," Dr. O'Flannel said, "but there's been a fair bit of auld chat in the village since you came back, about how it was you managed to have a baby at 52, after having been married for so long with no children at all? Was it that new fertility pill you took when you were up in Dublin, or was it all that goat's milk and cheese your husband was always so partial to?"

"Well, sure enough he did eat a lot of goat's cheese and he drank lots of goat's milk, but I really think it must have been the injection of live goat hormones he got at the Dublin Sex and Rejuvenation Clinic. Anyhow, our son Billy is outside in the waiting room. Maybe you'd like to just say hello if you have a minute to spare?"

"Well hello young man, and how are you today?" enquired the doctor.

"Not ba...aaaa...dd," said Billy.

The New Believer

The new parish priest had returned to Ireland after a stint with the Foreign Mission in Africa. During his time abroad he had become accustomed to doing Baptisms by total immersion.

He had arranged to perform a Baptism on an English Protestant who had decided to convert to Catholicism after living in Ireland for a number of years. It was the middle of winter and the priest had to break the ice on top of a holy well.

"Do you believe?", the priest shouted as the near frozen and drowned Englishman gasped for breath.

"Yes...Yes, I do believe..." he spluttered through chattering teeth.

"What do you believe?" The priest shouted, pushing his head under the water for the second time. Fighting to get away from the priest he managed to gasp,

"I do believe... you... are trying ...to drown me."

An Irish Toast

"Here's to the many happy hours I spent in the arms of another man's wife. Ladies and gentlemen, my Mother!"

The Drunken Driver

Murphy was driving his car along a country lane when he accidentally hit Bishop O'Flaherty's car coming in the opposite direction. Both cars were travelling about thirty miles an hour but the bishop's smaller car was knocked off the road and the poor bishop was thrown out into the roadside ditch. Murphy, who was relatively unharmed in his Mercedes, rushed up to the bishop, who lay there moaning, and offered him a drink from a bottle of Jameson's whiskey he had in his hand. The bishop took another and another and another until he was feeling quite merry. After a while he noticed he was drinking alone.

"Will you not take a wee drink with me yourself ?" he asked.

"I hate to drink alone, and after all, it's your Jameson's I'm drinking."

"No, Father," replied the very sober Murphy, "I've telephoned the local police station and reported the accident. The Police are on their way right now, and I'm not going to drink a drop until after we've both been breathalyzed."

Nicer Than Limerick Ham

A   Catholic priest and a Jewish rabbi struck up a conversation when they met in an otherwise empty railway carriage. After a   while the priest opened a package of ham sandwiches and teasingly offered one to the rabbi. The rabbi politely declined, but the priest continued to tempt him.

"You don't know what you're missing," he said. "Limerick ham is one of the finest tasting hams in the world. Just try one little taste. Your secret will be safe with me."

Again the rabbi politely declined, but confessed that he had tasted ham once as a boy and still remembered what it tasted like. Eventually they reached their destination and as they were parting, the rabbi said,

"Give your wife a kiss and a cuddle from me in bed tonight Father." And the priest replied,

"I don't have a wife and I've certainly never cuddled or kissed a woman." The rabbi smiled and said,

"Well Father, speaking from experience, I can tell you that kissing and cuddling one's wife in bed, is a lot nicer than any slice of Limerick ham."

Pancakes and Pizza

Tristram telephoned his friend Sebastian from the hospital ward where he was confined and said,

"Sebastian, be a dear boy, and telephone the matron for me. The old battle axe refuses to tell me what my ailment is and gives me pancakes and pizza to eat for breakfast, pancakes and pizza for lunch, and more pancakes and pizza for dinner." So his friend telephoned the matron.

"What ward is your friend in?" she asked.

"He's in Ward 69."

"Oh, yes, I remember the case," replied the matron. "Your friend Tristram has H.A.G.S. Disease."

"What on earth is HAGS Disease?" Sebastian asked. And the matron said,

"HAGS is short for Herpes, AIDS, Gonorrhea and Syphilis. And pancakes and pizza are the only things flat enough to slip under the door of his room."

The First Slice of Ham

Goldburger was invited to be guest of honor at the twenty first birthday party of Murphy's youngest son. The entree consisted of boiled Limerick ham. The guest of honour is customarily offered the first slice of ham. But even as it was being offered, Murphy suddenly realised that his Jewish friend might be offended, and apologized for the lack of foresight.

"Oh that's alright," Goldburger said, "my father always used to say to me, `Marvin, my boy, may the first slice of ham you eat choke you'....and remembering what he said, I've been careful ever since to only eat the second slice."

Palm Sunday

It was Palm Sunday, and Father O'Flynn, who was noted for his good-natured humor, announced from the pulpit,

"After Mass today the ushers will be distributing palms at the church doors. Will all those members of the congregation who habitually leave immediately after Holy Communion and before the end of the Mass, please leave their names and addresses with the ushers, and palm leaves will be mailed directly to them."

The Same Old Sin

This elderly spinster went to Father O'Flynn for her confession. "Yes My child?" enquired the priest.

"I went to a Hunt Ball, Father, had one too many, met this tall, dark and handsome man who swept me completely off my feet. He plied me with champagne and afterwards he drove me in his Mercedes. Then he kissed me very passionately and then he....and, after that he..."

"Yes, yes, yes," said Father O'Flynn, "but tell me how many times did you and he actually do ah...?"

"Oh just that one time, Father" she said.

"I've never seen him or the Mercedes since".

"Wait a minute," Father O'Flynn said, "this confession sounds very familiar to me. Have you by any chance ever confessed it to me on a previous occasion?"

"Yes, Father," she said, "many times."

"But surely I forgave you the first time? There's no need to keep on reconfessing what you did once with that man."

"Yes, Father, I know that, father, but I'm still sinning because every time I think about it,I get pleasure out of it."

Mack (The Knife) Magee

Magee was up in court charged with grievous bodily harm. He admitted stabbing the defendant, Moriarty Mulligan but pleaded it was an accident.

"Yer honor," he said, "there I was standing on the corner of Mary Street, minding my own business and peeling an apple with my flick knife, when Mulligan accidentally backed on to my knife and stabbed himself."

"It sounds plausible enough," the judge commented, "but this is a case of a multiple stabbing, and I hardly think the court will believe that the plaintiff Mr. Mulligan would have accidentally backed on to your knife seventeen times."

The New Bathing Suit

Mrs. McTavish was telling her friend about her husband's mean streak.

"Finally, after 40 years of marriage, my Donald agreed to take me to the seaside for a holiday. When I told him it was time I had a new bathing suit, he said, 'What's wrong with the old one?' And when I showed it to him all he said was, 'Och away with ya woman. It only needs a darn in the knees and it'll be good as new.'"

Eggs For Sex

When Mack (The Knife) Magee got out of prison he was very upset when his wife confessed that she had been unfaithful. "But I never took money from any of them," she assured him. "All I asked was that they put two fresh eggs in the basket." Magee rushed to the basket and counted four eggs and $300.00. Naturally he was pleased there were only four eggs, but he asked why she also had $300,00 in the basket. "Each time I had a dozen eggs," she said, "I sold them."

The Golfer's Magnifying Glasses

This fellow was a marvellous golfer, even though he suffered from two physical handicaps. First, he was so small in height that he could barely see over the top of his golf bag and second, he was so terribly short-sighted that whenever he played golf he had to wear specially-made glasses with lenses that measured half an inch thick. After a particularly brilliant game, and over a few drinks in the Clubhouse Bar, one of his companions asked him if he would reveal the secret of his success. The little golfer with the thick glasses finished his drink and said,

"The secret is in the glasses. They make everything look ten times bigger than it really is. I see the golf ball as big as a football, and the end of my iron or wood, looks as big as a tennis racquet. And as for the actual hole, I see that as big and as round as a builders cement bucket. Apart from that I am a very positive thinker and I think big." Shortly afterwards he went to the washroom and when he returned his friends noticed that the front of his pants were all wet.

"My God," the one said, "whatever happened to you in there?'

"I took off my glasses to have a pee," he confided. "And after I undid my zip and pulled out my willie, I knew it wasn't mine because it looked so small, so I put it back in my trousers again, and that was when I wet myself."

Brother McGinty

Patrick McGinty failed as a farmer and decided he had a late vocation for the priesthood. He entered a Trappist Monastery in Maynooth, Co.Kildare.

"It's kinda tough in here McGinty," the Abbot said, "you will have to take a vow of silence like the rest of us, and you will only be allowed to speak two words every ten years." Ten years went by and McGinty was summoned by the Abbot.

"Any complaints Brother McGinty?" he enquired. Using

the permitted two words, McGinty simply said,

"Bad food." The Abbot promised to do something about it and another ten years went by. The Abbot asked if he was now happy.

"Hard bed," McGinty replied. Another ten years went by and as McGinty stood before him for the third time, the Abbot said,

"What is it this time Brother McGinty?"

"I quit," said McGinty.

"Maybe it's just as well," replied the Abbot, "because in the thirty years you have been here, all I've ever heard you do is bitch, bitch, bitch."

The General And The Bishop

A bishop and a general caught sight of the other as they stood on the platform at Dublin's Westland Row Station waiting for the train. Twenty years had elapsed since they

were stationed at the Curragh Camp in County Kildare, and even though the Colonel was now a General and the camp Chaplain had become a Bishop, recognition was instant. Each immediately recalled his intense dislike for the other. The Bishop, pretending that he hadn't recognized the General, raised his hand and in a loud voice, insultingly addressed the General,

"I say porter," he said, "is this the Limerick train?"

The Colonel slowly looked the fat Bishop up and down before retorting, just as sarcastically,

"Yes it is Madame, but should you be travelling in your condition?"

Searching For A Pony

The poor teenage boy from the City Orphanage had been selected to spend a weekend on a stud farm. It was his first visit to the country and he knew nothing at all about animals. Early one morning the head groom was astonished to find the boy digging frantically in one of the stables with a pitchfork in his hands.

"You'll not find a crock of gold buried in there son," he kindly remarked.

"I'm not looking for a crock of gold," the boy said, "but with all this manure about, there's got to be a pony in here somewhere."

Mental Cruelty

This young girl left Ireland, went to England fell in love with an Englishman, got married and got pregnant several times. However the marriage was not a happy one and she sued her English husband for divorce, citing mental cruelty. She told the court that he wasn't very articulate and that he had only spoken to her three times in all the years they were married. She won her case and the judge also granted her custody of her three children.

Money Talk

Shay had been walking out with Mae for twenty years without even a hint of a marriage. Shay's excuse was that he hadn't enough money to keep himself, let alone a wife. He put it like this, "Dey do be after sayin' dat money talks an' cow muck walks, and mebee dat's why I'm rollin' in d'wan, an' dudder wan kapes sayin' goodbye."

Manana in Gaelic

A professor of languages from Madrid University was visiting one of his colleagues at The Dublin School of Languages.

"Tell me," said the Spanish professor, "is there a word in Gaelic similar to the Spanish manana?"

"To be sure there is," was the reply, "except the Gaelic word doesn't have quite the same sense of urgency."

The Two Irish Export Salesmen

A manure salesman and a cement salesman were sent on an overseas export mission to Africa. They got lost in the Sahara Desert and were desperately in need of food and water. The strongest one agreed to venture off alone in search of an oasis. He came back after several days and said, "There's good news and there's bad news. The bad news is that there's nothing out there but heaps of sand and camel dung. The good news is that there's tons of the stuff."

A Letter from Laura

Dear Mom and Dad,

I've got some bad news and some good news.

The bad news is that I fell off the back of my boyfriend's motorcycle and broke my arm, my collar bone, all my teeth and both legs. The doctors say I'll be in a wheelchair for the rest of my life. The good news is that I didn't lose the baby!

Yes! The baby! I'll bet that's a big surprise? I really didn't want to get pregnant but I got stoned after Obdedongo, that's the name of my boyfriend, gave me some Nembutal pills and a snort of his cocaine. Obedongo used to work as an exotic dancer and stripper at The Pink Elephant Club. One night, a little old lady got over-excited and tried to rip off his G string. Obedongo hit her over the head with his handbag and they fired him so he's now on Social Security. I confess I am just a little bit worried because after we made love last night, he told me he thinks he might be HIV positive. He didn't catch whatever it is off me! He probably caught it sharing a needle with his friends Tristram and Sebastian. But I am fine. Really I am. And I don't have any spots or anything like that. I have managed to get a job working nights at a nearby slaughterhouse. They let me sit in my own wheelchair but I know I'll have to stop work soon because of the baby. I get so very, very tired. Obedongo asked me to write and ask you for an immediate loan. Can you make it $500.00? I wouldn't ask, but we got a bit behind with the rent and the landlord says he is going to throw us and our bed out in the street if we don't have the money by Friday.

Your loving daughter,
Laura.
P.S. There's more! Please read the next page...

---- 🍀 ----

Hi Mom. Hi Dad.

I have to confess that I am neither pregnant nor crippled. I am not a substance abuser and I don't have a boyfriend called Obedongo. However I do have some bad news. I have failed my accountancy exams. Professor Hanratty says I would have made a very incompetent CPA anyway and he thinks I might do better at Psychology or Creative Writing. I know how terribly disappointed you must be but I sincerely hope that the story I made up will somehow enable you to appreciate that there are worse things in life than failing an exam. Your ever-loving daughter,

Laura.

P.P.S. Can I still come home for the holidays?

Skinny Dipping

A little old spinster lady bought the penthouse apartment in the block overlooking the sea. She wrote to the town clerk, and all the borough executives, complaining about the nude men exposing themselves and unashamedly cavorting about and boldly flaunting themselves in the 'Men Only' bathing place in front of her apartment block. They made an appointment and all went to visit her at her apartment.

"Madam," the borough surveyor said, "we were particularly careful to ensure that there would be no planning objections regarding this block. That's why we made the contractor build an eight-foot-high wall around the men's bathing place. We have examined your complaint, but we fail to see any of those naked men you claim to be able to see."

"You can see them," she insisted, "if you put this chair on top of the table, climb up, and use these binoculars."

The Price of Virtue

Murphy found himself alone with a lovely girl in a railway carriage. He tried to ignore her at first but the smell of her 'Georgio' perfume was so evocative that even though he appeared to be reading 'The Irish Times', he was secretly turned on. He noticed her tight-fitting silk blouse and the way her boobs stuck out like a couple of Sugar Loaf mountain tops. Greedily his eyes took in her black leather skirt which was split to the top of her thigh. He noticed her lovely long legs, her anklet chain, her brightly-painted long nails, her high heeled shoes, her creamy skin, the crimson curve of her moist pouting lips, the provocative way she kept crossing and uncrossing her legs, and the rhythmic way in which she kept slipping her foot in and out and up and down in her black patent shoes. After a while he could stand it no longer, and putting down his newspaper, he leaned across toward her and said,

"Pardon me miss, but would you be willing to have dinner with me this evening? We could share a bottle of Dom Perignon, take in a show at the Abbey Theatre, and afterwards we could go back to hotel? I would be willing to give you as much as $50.00 in cash for your services?"

"Cheeky thing," she coldly retorted, "I'm not interested."

"Would you be interested if I were to increase my offer from $50 to $500.00?"

"Now you're talking," she said.

"How about accepting $75.00?" he ventured.

"Definitely not," she haughtily replied. "What do you think I am?"

"Miss," he said, "we have already established just what you are, and now we are haggling over the price."

The London Sloan Street Ranger

Caroline went to the cinema with her boy friend Henry and sat in the back row. During the interval when the lights came on, Caroline noticed her friend Natasha walking up the aisle, and how embarrassed Natasha looked when her panties fell down around her ankles. Caroline laughed and laughed, because she knew hers were safe in her handbag.

The Old Bull and the Young Bull

"Oh, look," said the young bull, "there's a whole herd of cows in the next field. Why don't we charge over right now and give one a good bonking?"

"Steady on lad," said the old bull, "I've got a better idea. Why don't we stroll over, and bonk them all?"

The Golf Pro And The Priest

"Fancy a game of golf, Father?" the club professional said, adding with his tongue in his cheek, "I'm still learning how to play myself." Father O'Flynn who had just joined the club readily agreed. Just before teeing off, the lying pro slyly said,

"Let's make it interesting Father. How about playing for money?" Father O'Flynn agreed and he got taken for a cool $50.00.

"Tough luck, Father, "the pro said, "Perhaps I should have mentioned I am the club pro. However, I hope we can play again soon, but in the meantime if there is anything I can do for you here at the club, let me know?"

"Thank you for the offer," replied Father O'Flynn, "but I'd rather not play with you again. And to show you there's no hard feelings, if I should ever meet your father and mother, I'd be happy to marry them."

♣

Strippers At The Club

Casey anxiously telephoned his wife and said,

"I'm phoning you from the Over Sixties Club. I knew it was a 'men only' night, but honest to God, I didn't expect there would be four sexy fat strippers showing off all their personal belongings, and surprise surprise, guess what? I've got this sudden urge to have sex. What do you think I should do?"

"If you think there's anything you can do, Pat," she said "get in your car right away, and come home as fast as you can."

Bula-Bula

The priest from the Irish-Africa Foreign Mission had obtained permission from the tribal chief and was about the preach his first sermon to the thousands of black people who had assembled and were seated on the brown baked earth of the African kraal.

"The great white chief has sent me," the priest shouted as loudly as he could," and I bring you gifts of candy bars and bags of M & M sweeties. I bring you gifts of glass necklaces and shiny beads from Woolworth's. I bring you good news ...."

"Bula-Bula," they shouted, interrupting him. Patiently he waited for all the shouting and cheering to stop, and when everyone had become quiet once again, he continued,

"I bring you brotherly love and friendship from all the white people in the world to all the black people. Truly we want nothing in return, not your ivory, not your cattle, not your trees, not your lands. All we come for is your hand in friendship..."

"Bula-Bula," they screamed, and now the whole crowd went wild. Some were even frothing at the mouth with sheer joy and excitement. Collectively they were so over-come that the whole congregation stood up and began to beat wildly on their shields with their long spears. The missionary priest was too overcome to continue. Humbly be bowed his head in prayer and then he thanked them all for their warm reception. As he turned to go, the chief showed him the short cut around the back of the kraal where the tribe's animals were quartered, and said, "Mind you don't step in the Bula-Bula."

The Cat On The Roof

Gilhooly lived with his wife, his widowed mother and his beloved cat. He had to go away on business and after a few days he telephoned his wife.

"How are things?"he enquired.

"The cat's dead," she said abruptly.

"Oh, that's terrible bad news, "Gilhooly said "but you might have broken the news a bit better."

"How would you have put it?" his wife asked.

"I would have wrapped it up a bit and gradually eased into it. I would have said something to the effect that the cat had chased a mouse up on to the roof, and that the roof was wet and slippery, and that the cat fell off, was rushed to the vet's for surgery, had an operation, and that even though the vet did his best, the poor cat died after a brave struggle."

A couple of days later he telephoned again and said,

"How are things?" And his wife said,

"Your mother was up on the roof......"

The Sad Second Husband

As the sexton at Glasnevin Cemetery in Dublin was tending to his business, he came across a very dejected-looking man dressed all in black. Tears rolled down the mans face as he sobbed uncontrollably in front of a large marble headstone.

"Why did you have to go?", he moaned, "Why did you have to go?"

"Time is a great healer," said the sexton, "but still and all, it's hard being a widower."

"I'm not a widower," replied the mourner, "It's my wife's first husband that's buried here."

Praying And Acting

Casey and Murphy found themselves in a field being chased by a bull. They ran like hell but the bull seemed to be gaining on them.

"Let's stop running, lie down and pray to God that the bull thinks we're dead," Casey said.

"You try it and see if it works," Murphy replied, "But I'll do my praying while I'm running."

Converting the Cannibals

The Christian Brother addressed the school class.

"What's the first thing our Irish missionary priests have to do when they come face-to-face with a tribe of hungry cannibals?"

One little hand shot up.

"Yes Liam, please tell us?" said the Christian Brother.

"The Priests have to first convert them into vegetarians."

Outrunning A Bear

Casey and Murphy went prospecting for gold in California. They were asleep in their cabin when Casey heard a banging on the door. He looked out of the window and saw a huge bear trying to break in. He woke Murphy and said,

"Better get the hell out of here PDQ. There's a huge bear

smashing down the front door." Murphy jumped up and sat down again to put his Reeboks on. Casey said,

"Forget the running shoes Mick. You'll never outrun the bear anyway." And Murphy said, "I don't have to outrun the bear. I only have to outrun you."

Sign Language

A deaf and dumb man went into a hardware store, banged his fist on the counter, pointed to his thumb-nail, made another hitting motion with his right fist, raised ten fingers, then raised two more, and finally opened his thumb and forefinger about three inches. The assistant nodded his head, went away and came back with a hammer and a dozen three-inch nails. The deaf and dumb man left with his purchase feeling very pleased. Shortly afterwards a blind man came in. He wanted to buy a scissors. How do you think he communicated his wishes to the assistant? He asked him!

Sex Rejuvenation Pills

Two farmers were chatting about their livestock and one said, "My old bull has gone right off it these days and hasn't serviced a cow in over a month."

"Mine had the same problem," the other said, "but I went to that new vet in the village and he gave me these wonderful pills. I only had to give one to the bull and he immediately set about servicing every cow in the paddock twice a day."

"That's wonderful. What's the name of those pills as I'd also like to get some for my bull?" And the other one said,

"I forget the name, but they're white, and they are round, and they measure about a quarter of an inch thick - and they taste of peppermint."

The Ladies Only Chain Letter

Are you in a rut? Could you be happier? Would you like to have a little bit more fun and romance in your life?

The lady who originally wrote these words is a lady just like you. She started a chain letter for Ladies Only in West Palm Beach, on New Year's Day, January, 1992. To date, she has succeeded in bringing new joy and happiness to over one million ladies, who feel they have been used and abused by the men in their lives.

To change your life for the better, make a copy of this letter, write your own name and address at the bottom of the list, and send it to five of your friends, who are equally as unhappy as yourself. Then send your unwanted husband or lover to the first name on your list.

When your own name comes to the top of the list, you will receive a total of 13,500 men, one of whom is bound to be better than the man you now have.

Breaking the chain can sometimes bring bad luck. One lady who broke the chain got her own husband back!

Age is relatively unimportant. A 78-year-old-lady joined just three months ago and although she's now passed away, she received as many as 195 men the week before she died. The undertaker claimed it took him seven hours just to get the smile off her face.

High-Pressure Selling

All the neighbors knew that Paddy McGinty was poor and that he only had one cow. Consequently they were very surprised when he invited them to come and look at his new automatic milking machine.

"I kept telling the sales representative that I only had one cow and no money, but he was a fantastic salesman and tempted me with a wonderful offer. He gave me a 50% discount, and took the cow in part exchange."

A Couple of Naughty Girl's Names

Pat and Mike went to confession and Mike went in first.

"I committed the mortal sin of fornication with one of the village girls," said Mike.

"How many times?" Father O'Flynn enquired.

"Just the once with this particular girl, Father."

"Has she come to confession with you?" he asked.

"No, Father."

"What's the name of the girl?" enquired the priest.

"I had to promise I'd never reveal it, Father" Mike said.

"Was it young Susie Shananegin?" Father O'Flynn asked.

"No, Father."

"Was it that bold Madge Magee from over the mountain?"

"No, Father."

"You are truly sorry though, aren't you, my son?"

"Aye, I am that, Father," he said.

"I absolve you, but try not to do it again. Now make a good Act of Contrition and for your penance say Ten Glory Be's, Ten Our Father's and Ten Hail Mary's."

"What did he give you, Mike?" Pat anxiously asked his friend when he came out of the confession box.

"Ten Glory Be's, Ten Hail Mary's. Ten Our Father's and the names of 2 more naughty local girls."

Good Mannered Gilda

Gilda and Golda hadn't seen each other for about twenty years and Gilda said,

"What's new?"

"My Abe is such a mensch," Golda confided. "Just feast your eyes on this huge 3 carat diamond ring and the gold chain he just bought me for our anniversary."

"Fantastic" said Gilda as Golda went on,

"The mink coat he bought me last year. The pearl necklace he bought the year before. I got my beautiful tan in Majorca. We were there for a month you know."

"Fantastic," Gilda said. And Gilda continued,

"We spend such a lot of time abroad in our beautiful penthouse apartment in Palma. It's right on the Paseo Maritemo you know, in the very best position and so near to everything. I look out a window and I can see the marina and our beautiful 40' yacht. I look out another window and I see my beautiful big series 7 BMW. "

"Fantastic," Gilda said.

"Of course I've still got the 560SL Merc.," Golda said, and as an afterthought added,

" And what have you been up to, if anything?"

"I've been to a finishing school in Switzerland," Gilda said.

"Finishing school," exclaimed Gilda, "What ever did they teach you?" Gold smiled sweetly and very quietly said,

"They taught me to say Fantastic instead of Bullshit."

Limerick Ham

Seamus Shananegin had been confined to bed for some time and even though he had recently had quadruple by-pass surgery, the doctor finally confided to Mrs. Shananegin that the future looked bleak.

"How long has he got left doctor?" she anxiously enquired, "and shall I keep him on a low fat, low salt diet?"

"Well," said the doctor, "let's put it this way. Just don't think about buying him any green bananas. But sure it doesn't matter much what he eats now. Give him anything at all he fancies, and maybe it's best not to tell him the sad news? He's so frail the shock might well kill him before his time?" So Mrs. Shananegin went out and bought all the things she knew her husband liked to eat.

"Seamus," she said, "the doctor says you can eat anything at all you like. Isn't that good news? There you are now, sit up and eat your fill of this lovely meal of fried eggs, fried black pudding, fried sausage, fried tomatoes and look, there's even a bit of fried bread as well. Isn't that grand now?"

"Aye, 'tis grand," Seamus said, "but you know what I really fancy? I fancy a cut off that lovely looking Limerick ham you just bought."

"Darlin'," she said, "can't I tempt you with another egg or maybe another couple of pieces of bacon instead? You see,I was trying to save the ham until after the funeral."

The Ambidextrous Golfer

The newest member of the club had no one to play with, so the Captain told him he would be happy to play with him and that he that he was free for a game at ten o'clock each morning for the next three days.

"Ten o'clock precisely," the Captain reminded him, "except you are not to worry should I be two or three minutes late." The Captain turned up at precisely ten o'clock for the following three days. The new member observed that the Captain played left-handed on the first day. On the second day he was astonished to note that he played right-handed. But to cap it all, he noticed that on the third day the Captain had switched back to playing left-handed.

"How come," he at last ventured, "that some days you play left- handed and other days you play right-handed?'

"I take my golf very seriously indeed," replied the Captain. "But I am also a very superstitious man. I believe in signs and omens. For instance, each morning when I wake up, I look at the way my wife is sleeping, and if she is lying on her left side, I play left-handed, and if she is lying on her right side, then I play right-handed."

"But what happens if she's lying on her back?" enquired the new member. The Captain smiled and said,

"Ah. That's when I'm two or three minutes late."

The Singing Telegram

A smartly dressed young man wearing a fancy post office uniform knocked on Mrs. Shananegin's door on her 70th birthday and handed her a telegram.

"Ah, a singing telegram," she said, "how wonderful. I've never had one of them. Go on then. Open it up and sing it for me."

"It's not intended to be a singing telegram," he said "and it is marked Private and Personal. I think you should open it."

"Oh, please" she begged. "This is my 70th birthday. Make an old lady happy. You open it and sing it for me please." The young man cleared his throat, opened the telegram and sang,

"Da-ra-te-tum-te-tum. Fred and the kids are dead."

Vinyl Floor Covering

Miss Appropriate went into a carpet shop that also sold vinyl floor coverings and asked to see some different colors and patterns.

"Something in a small pattern, perhaps with some green and earth tone colors" she said. The sales assistant unrolled fifty rolls of vinyl for her inspection. Finally, Miss Appropriate said,

"I think I like the first one you showed me best."

"Thank you madame," the assistant said, "Shall we make an appointment now for one of our consultants to come and measure up, or do you know how many yards or square metres you require?"

"Oh, I only want a piece big enough to cover the floor of my canary's cage," she said.

Cherokee Murphy

Murphy was crazy about the old wild west, so he travelled to America, visited an Indian reservation and asked the Cherokee Chief if he could live as an Indian with the tribe.

"We'll accept you if you can pass the triple test," the Chief said. "The first thing you have to do is drink a pint of Jack Daniels in one go. Then we give you a Winchester rifle with only one bullet, and you have to go into the mountains and shoot a grisly bear between the eyes. The third thing you have to do, is make love to the oldest, fattest and ugliest unmarried woman in the tribe." Murphy drank the pint of Jack Daniels, took the rifle and staggered off toward the mountains. Three days later he returned still a bit bleary-eyed from the whiskey and looking like he'd been in a fight, and lost. His face was clawed and bleeding. Half his hair was torn out. His clothes were dirty and hanging off him in shreds. "Right," Murphy said to the Cherokee Chief, "now where's this ugly fat old woman I've got to shoot between the eyes?"

The Warm Diamond Ring

Goldburger had just bought his wife a very large diamond ring. She was wearing it at her nephew's bar mitzvah party, but nobody noticed it until she loudly announced,

"Oh, I do think it's so warm in here wearing my new ring."

The Ring With The Curse

""Your ring is simply gorgeous, Mrs. Goldburger," a friend commented on noticing her huge diamond ring.

"Yes," replied Mrs. Goldburger, "it really is gorgeous but a terrible curse goes with it."

"What kind of curse?" the neighbor asked. Mrs. Goldburger sighed deeply and said,

"Mr. Goldburger."

A Cure For Migraine

Murphy turned up late for work every day for a week. The following week, one of his bosses, Mr. Flim, said that if he persisted in being late he would be fired. Murphy explained that he had been suffering with a bad migraine. Flim listened sympathetically and said,

"Whenever I get a bad headache I go to bed with my wife no matter what time it is. She lets me put my head between her breasts, then she very gently massages the back of my neck, and in less than five minutes the headache's gone completely. It works every time for me and I can highly recommend it."

Murphy said he was prepared to try anything. He was on time every day for the following week. On Friday when he was giving him his wages, Flim said,

"How's the head?"

"Fine," said Murphy, "I took your advice and followed your recommendations exactly. The migraine goes away in a few minutes every time. And I would like to say, I think your wife has lovely breasts and wonderful healing hands."

A Last Request

The doctor looked at Gilhooly and shook his head.

"I'm going to give it to you straight," he said. "It's bad news, I'm afraid. I've done all I can and you'll probably die within the next twenty four hours. Is there anything at all you would like to have? Any last requests? If there is anything at all, please let me know?'

"There is just one thing I really would like doctor," whispered the very worried Gilhooly, "and it's a second opinion."

The Snake Oil Salesman

The snake oil salesman at the Kerry fair was loudly proclaiming his miracle cure for old age to anyone who would listen. He told the crowd that had gathered around his tent,

"A thousand years ago Osian himself brought this cure back from Tir Na N'Og - that fabled land where nobody ever gets old - and it's been handed down from generation to generation in my family. My own mother took a spoonful of this magic medicine every day of her life and she lived to be one hundred and thirty-nine. I'm her youngest son and I'm one hundred and five."

"Is he really as old as he claims he is?" a member of the crowd asked his young assistant.

"I don't really know," was the reply, "I've only worked for him for the last eighty eight years."

No Sex Allowed

"There's good news and there's bad news Mrs. Hanratty," Dr. O'Flannel said. "The good news is that your husband could live to a ripe old age with plenty of TLC. But the bad news is that any kind of sexual excitement would probably kill him. I know how much you love each other so it is going to hard for both of you. I suggest that he sleeps downstairs on the sofa bed and you sleep upstairs." Three months went by and Mrs. Hanratty couldn't stand the separation any longer. She got up in the middle of the night and started to go upstairs, when she met her husband coming down.

"I was just on my way down to commit suicide," he said.

"And I was just coming up to murder you," she replied.

The Prostitute

Brendan wrote home telling his mother he would be coming home from London for the holidays and bringing his new English fiancee.

"I would like to make a good first impression, mother" he said in his letter, "so try to tidy things up a bit. Perhaps you can have the cottage white washed, chase the auld hens out of the kitchen and maybe wash the pig with some pine disinfectant?" They were all sitting down to afternoon tea with buttered scones, when the mother leaned across towards the heavily-painted and flashily-dressed girl, and said,

"And what did you do in London before you met my darlin' boy Brendan?"

"I was a prostitute," the girl said.

"There you are now," said the mother, offering the girl another scone before adding,

"I'm afraid I've got a bit deaf in one ear. What was that you said you were?"

"Prostitute," said the girl, "I used to be a prostitute."

"Thanks be to God," the mother said, "for a terrible moment, I thought you said you were a Protestant."

The Mercenary Poker Players

Four keen poker players had been meeting regularly in each other's homes, to play cards, and over the years had become good friends. One night when they were playing one guy seemed to have more than his share of luck and as chance would have it, he died of a heart attack just as he was reaching out across the table to draw in his winnings.

Tom owed him $100.00. Dick owed him $200.00 and Harry owed him $300. They were so shocked at the time that each one inadvertently picked up his own stake and pocketed it. On the day of the funeral as they watching their old friend's coffin being slowly lowered into the ground, each felt a touch of remorse over the uncollected debt. Believing that their old friend would rest more peaceably, Tom opened his wallet and in a generous gesture threw his $100.00 in cash on top of the coffin. Dick opened his wallet and tossed in his $200.00 in cash. Meanwhile Harry, who had been busy writing out a cheque said to his two friends,

"Look fellas, between us we owed him $600.00 right? So I am putting in my personal check for the full amount of $600.00 and since I'll be needing some change, I'll simply take out the $300 in cash you fellas put in, and that makes us all square."

Kinky Sex

Murphy went to see Dr. O'Flannel and said,

"I think my girl friend is kinky, and I was wondering if we could have sex in your office while you watch, and perhaps you can give her some of your professional advice?"

"It's a bit unusual," Dr. O'Flannel said, "how long is it going to take?"

"About a quarter of a hour."

"I'll have to charge $35.00 for up to half an hour," the doctor said. Murphy agreed and made a 7 o'clock evening appointment for the following Thursday. They lay on Dr. O'Flannel's couch, and had sex while he watched, he said, "I saw nothing kinky,"

"I'd like you to see it again," Murphy said, "Can we make another appointment for the same time next week?" The doctor agreed. He watched them have sex the second time, and again said, that he saw nothing kinky.

"Even so," said Murphy, "I'd still like to make another appointment for next Thursday evening." Dr. O'Flannel said,

"Now hold your horses, Mike. Something funny is going on. What's the game?" And Murphy said,

"The problem is that my girl friend and I are married to two other people. A room at the Holiday Inn costs $75.00 a night, and a room at the Hilton costs $100.00. You only charge $35.00, and I can claim 80% of that back off Medicare."

Stuck On The Golf Course

Casey was teaching a young woman how to hold a golf club. He put his arms around her from behind and held both her hands and the golf club with his. At the same time he happened to look down, and noticing that his pants zipper was undone, he let go of her hands to pull his zipper, but it got caught in the back of her dress.

"If we stick very close together," he said, "and we walk slowly back to the clubhouse, with you in front and me behind, nobody will notice, and maybe I'll be able to borrow a pair of pliers to help get us unstuck." But on the way back a dog saw them, and threw a bucket of water over them.

The Little Sparrow

A little sparrow lived in a beautiful tree deep in the forest and she was so happy that she sang all day long. She fell in love with a young male sparrow who lived in the next tree. Together they built a new nest and were very happy. But one day her mate died and the little sparrow found herself left all alone. She didn't quite know what to do or how to cope. She stopped singing and began to cry. All she did every day was cry and cry. But it only seemed to make things worse and so she became quite depressed and withdrawn. As time went by, the nights grew cold and Autumn soon turned into Winter.

By this time all of the other sparrows had flown South in search of food and warmer weather. But the little sparrow refused to fly South with them and chose to remain mournfully in her nest. Then the snow came and with it the cruel North Wind. It blew the nest away and the poor little sparrow was without food and shelter of any kind, and so she grew colder and colder and thinner and thinner.

Eventually she managed to find refuge in a barn along with several cattle. One of the cows dumped on her and while she didn't like it, it was at least warm and so she began to feel better and better. She became quite cheerful and began to sing again. A large cat heard her singing, went into the barn, dug her out of the cow muck, and ate her.

On reflection, someone who shits on you is not necessarily your enemy, and someone who gets you out of the shit is not necessarily your friend either. So if there's a moral to the story, it must be that if you're happy in a pile of shit, you had better keep your mouth shut.

Sex Twice a Year

Casey was telling a friend about his rotten bad luck. He said,

"My eldest son lost his job. My youngest son is an alcoholic and can't work. My daughter's husband has left her and she and her four kids are coming to live with us. But worst of all, after being married for nearly forty years my wife's suddenly turned into a raving nympho. She's now demanding sex twice a year."

The Nymphomaniacs Conference

Goldburger was flying to London and was seated next to a very attractive young woman.

"I'm going to a rag trade conference," he confided.

"Mine's a business trip too," she said. "I'm a nymphomaniac and I'm the keynote speaker at a nymphomaniacs conference."

"Oy, yoi," Goldburger said giving her the glad eye, "I suppose you've had sex with lots of men from many different countries?"

"Yes", she said, "and without a doubt the world's greatest lovers are the firey, hot-tempered Celts from Scotland and Ireland. By the way, my name's Cynthia, but you can call me Cyn for short. What's your name?" And Goldburger said,

"Jock McMurphy."

Need Extra Copies For Your Friends? Call Toll-Free Anytime And Use Your

6